Man's Best Hope

MAN'S BEST HOPE

Roland B. Gittelsohn

Random House · New York

Second Printing, June 1966

© Copyright, 1961, by Roland B. Gittelsohn
All rights reserved under International and Pan-American Copyright
Conventions. Published in New York by Random House, Inc., and
simultaneously in Toronto, Canada, by Random House of Canada
Limited.
Library of Congress Catalog Card Number: 61-14892
Manufactured in the United States of America

To My
Beloved Children
—David
—Judith
—Richard
And to Ruth

There are only two kinds of people left in the world. The one group is intelligent, but lacking in faith. The other has faith but is lacking in intelligence.

Abu'l Ala

I saw in my time many of the believers clinging to unsound doctrine and mistaken beliefs, while many of those who deny the faith boast of their unbelief and despise men of truth. . . .

Saadya Gaon

A WORD OF GRATITUDE

How can one even begin to thank all those whose friendship and assistance have made a book of this kind possible? At the top of any list would have to come the students—high school, college and adult—whose perplexities and challenges have activated my religious thinking during the thirty-five years since I faced my first class as a teacher.

Among individuals no one deserves more gratitude than my beloved Ruth, who repaid the neglect and abuse suffered by every writer's wife with endless encouragement and help. Many errors of fact and infelicities of expression were removed from these pages by the following, who read the material with scrupulous care: Abraham Burack, George Russell Harrison, F. Alexander Magoun and Albert Vorspan.

The entire burden of typing and retyping my manuscript

was carried cheerfully as an extracurricular task by my devoted secretary, Bessie R. Berman.

These sentences cannot encompass more than the smallest part of my appreciation to all of them. I hope they are aware of the wide margin by which my gratitude exceeds my power of expression.

Roland B. Gittelsohn

Chestnut Hill, Massachusetts
April, 1961

Contents

Man's Best Hope

I

Introduction by Paradox

On the face of it there would appear to be ample reason for religious leaders in our time and place to rejoice. All the barometers of religious zeal seem to be rising. A century ago only twenty Americans of each hundred were affiliated with a church. By 1958 the proportion had risen to sixty-three percent, constituting a total of more than one hundred nine million church members. In the past thirty years, while population in this country was increasing by forty percent, religious affiliation doubled. It is reported that the American people are now spending in the neighborhood of two billion dollars per year on organized religion; building costs alone in 1958 exceeded eight hundred fifty million dollars. The Broadcasting Film Commission of the National Council of Churches, responsible for preparing religious television materials for most of our Protestant Churches, was budgeted to spend just short of three million dollars in 1959.

In 1957 the number of Roman Catholic church members in the United States increased by nearly a million. Over seven million children were reported enrolled in Catholic parochial schools or in special religious classes during released time. In the very short period since the close of World War II, the Union of American Hebrew Congregations, representing American Reform Judaism, has doubled both the number of its constituent congregations and the individual families in them. This rate of growth has been paralleled by Conservative and Orthodox Judaism.

One of the most dramatic scenes of increased religious interest is that of our college campuses. Thirty years ago those few of us who were deeply concerned with religion as undergraduates found sparse and infrequent company. Except for an occasional Bible course and outside of denominationally sponsored colleges, formal instruction in religion was almost nonexistent. Today the picture has changed almost beyond belief. More colleges each year are sponsoring religious-emphasis days or weeks. The visiting clergymen who participate in these programs find encouraging evidence of student interest. Twenty years ago, twenty-one students were enrolled in Princeton University's first undergraduate course in religion; in 1956 the registration there in religion courses came to seven hundred. In 1936 the three courses in religion offered at Yale attracted fifty of the twenty-eight hundred students then registered. In 1956 the number of courses had grown to fourteen; out of four thousand students, five hundred were enrolled in them. A recent study sponsored by Cornell University reports that eighty percent of the seven thousand students interviewed on twelve campuses expressed a need for religion and that, in the single decade commencing in 1947, the number of colleges offering degrees in religion had increased from one hundred twenty-eight to three hundred and two.

Nor is such happy evidence limited to statistics. It is a rare Monday morning on which our newspapers fail to display photographs of the President of the United States chatting with the pastor or priest of whichever church he attended the preceding day. After six and a half decades of use in its original form, the pledge of allegiance to our national flag was amended to include the words "under God." In signing the act authorizing this change, President Eisenhower commented: "In this way we are reaffirming the transcendence of religious faith in America's heritage and future." Periodicals and publications which showed little or no interest in religious topics until a short time ago are now eager for material of this nature. More and more pressure is being exerted on public school educators to include religious emphases in their programs. Our professional advertisers now devote their best talent to an annual campaign for "religion in American life" in which all of us are urged to attend weekly the Religious Service of our choice. It is no longer uncommon to see trucks on the highways bearing, in addition to their commercial identity, some such inscription as "Let's all go to church this week!" Even our motion pictures and popular songs seem suddenly to have become agencies of religious persuasion.

So the evidence seems to mount that religion is coming into its own in the United States, that our civilization is strengthening its spiritual roots and our citizens are increasingly concerned with matters of ultimate destiny.

▼ *Never Look a Gift Horse . . .*

Does it appear picayune or captious to approach so pleasant a prospect with suspicion? To do otherwise would be, I fear, unforgivably shallow. For beneath these surface symptoms of success there is much to disturb.

True, the numbers of people affiliated with our synagogues and churches have greatly increased. But attendance at Services of Worship, though perceptibly greater than it was a few decades ago, has by no means kept pace. Except for such special occasions as Christmas and Easter among Christians or Rosh Hashana and Yom Kippur among Jews, and allowing for an occasional preacher of such popularity or eloquence that people come to hear him more than to pray actively themselves, our impressive religious auditoria are far from filled.

In 1948 Lincoln Barnett published the results of his survey on the religious beliefs and behavior of the American public. A comparison of affirmative answers to the following questions would probably be as disturbing today as it was then:

Do you believe in God?—95%
Do you belong to a synagogue or church?—76%
Do you attend Religious Services regularly?—41%
Do your religious beliefs have any effect on your ideas on politics and business?—39%*

Responses to the last of these questions suggest that religion is not accomplishing on the ethical front anything like the goals it professes to seek. There is ample additional evidence on this point. No one alert to reality can doubt that we suffer today from much more mental disease and emotional distress than did our fathers. Our divorce rates increase frighteningly despite the allegation that families which "pray together stay together." The incidence of both juvenile delinquency and adult crime is alarming. Many of those who are conspicuously identified with organized religion ex-

* *Ladies Home Journal*, November, 1948

hibit something less than a commendable ethic in their business or professional careers.

At the international level can we even pretend that peace is a more realistic prospect now than it was before the so-called revival of religion? Within our own nation, can we afford smugness when some of our leading church people are guilty of anti-Semitism and segregation of the Negro is defended scarcely less within the household of religion than outside it?

Some years ago the studies of Hartshorne and May, among others, demonstrated convincingly that standards of personal ethics were certainly no higher among the religiously affiliated than among the unaffiliated. More recently Gordon Allport, Harvard psychologist, has summarized the findings of several independent and reliable studies: ". . . many investigations show that on the average churchgoers and professedly religious people have considerably more prejudice than do non-churchgoers and non-believers."* Surely the gap among the churched between ethical promise and performance leaves no reason for the kind of complacency which our statistics of membership might otherwise induce.

Here, then, is the disquieting paradox from which our inquiry proceeds. On the one hand: enheartening evidence that more and more Americans are formally associating themselves with the agencies of religion. On the other: appalling reason to fear that the ideal goals of religion may be farther from our grasp than ever.

How shall we explain such contradiction?

▼ *Toward an Answer*

It would be foolish to assume that either a single or a simple explanation is possible. It would be grossly unfair,

* "Religion and Prejudice," *Crane Review*, Fall, 1959

moreover, to place the entire blame on religion. Surely a part at least of the paradox is explicable on the basis of our very human imperfection. Man's appetite for moral goodness has always exceeded his digestive capacity. We must not torment ourselves with guilt just because we are unable to achieve the ideal goals we are capable of envisaging. At man's present stage of development no religion, however appropriate or mature, can reasonably be expected to transform him into an angel.

Another part of the answer we seek inheres in the pressures and strains of a civilization which is sometimes too much for us. As I write these lines on the porch of a lake-front cottage in New Hampshire, a jet plane flying beyond the reach of vision breaks the sound barrier. Our little fox terrier is terrified by the booming echo which bounces back and forth across the lake. His nervous structure, adequate to carry him through most situations he must face, was neither meant nor prepared for the effects of speed faster than sound. My nervous system is not entirely different from his. Though my fright a moment ago was less than his, there are tensions caused by the achievements and possibilities of modern science for which I too am unprepared. No attempt to understand the malaise of our time will succeed even partially unless it takes this into account.

But when these and many other valid explanations have all been placed on the record, a large share of culpability remains for religion. Though we could in no event come even near ethical perfection, the right kind of religion should enable us to approach more closely than we have. This in turn would reduce some of the nearly unbearable strains we suffer. And those which would necessarily remain would be easier for us to handle if our religious ideas were more appropriate to the time in which we live.

The plain, palpable fact is that most of us today are operating with religious concepts which are tired and outworn.

We mouth familiar words, at times convincing ourselves that we understand and mean them, but their relevance to the issues and problems we face is more often than not obscure.

Too many of us have never grown up religiously. The spiritual concepts we express are still the very ones we acquired in childhood. We would have little regard for the adult whose taste in art had never advanced beyond what he believed to be beautiful when he was busy with kindergarten finger-painting. Or whose standards of sculptural excellence were arrested on the level of mud pies. Yet the average American adult—Christian and Jew alike—remains close to the religious level of his early childhood. His spiritual quotient is far from flattering.

So long as this remains true, it is vain to hope that religion will perform its proper and potential role either in alleviating our personal anxieties or in the making of a more just and righteous society.

A man I know spoke for many more than himself when he said one day: "My friends had a bogeyman to frighten them; I had God. Later I tried to compensate by thinking of God as a super Santa Claus."

How often this kind of arrested spiritual growth manifests itself in conversation with new acquaintances who eagerly volunteer the information that they are atheists! Again and again an hour or two with such a person establishes that he isn't an atheist at all. Indeed, we sometimes discover that his beliefs and mine are remarkably similar but that we express them in different vocabularies. He often proves to be not one who denies God, but who has quite properly rejected an idea of God long since outgrown, without ever having been introduced to a concept more compatible with adult intelligence.

I have come to believe through the years—with increasing firmness of conviction—that the greatest spiritual need of our generation is a new vocabulary for ancient and eternal truths, a concept of religion and God which will really function in our lives and the lives of our children.

This book springs from the fervent hope that I may have some modest contribution to make in that direction.

▼ Past and Future

Even in our modern world the notion that our concept of God is subject to change brings distress to some of us. Too often we forget that man's capacity to comprehend a tiny fringe of the ultimate has always changed and grown. The very concepts to which the more conservative among us cling so desperately today were once innovations, bitterly resented and resisted.

Only a fleeting glance at the past will suffice to indicate how true this is. Men once believed—men who were advanced, intelligent, sophisticated for their time—that every rock or tree housed a godlike spirit within it. It was a substantial shock for such men to be told somewhere along the line that the houses they had built for God were too small for Him. Other generations of men believed with equal fervor that idols were gods. When Abraham smashed the idols in his father's shop to demonstrate how false and shabby this concept was, we may be sure his temerity met with something less than enthusiastic acceptance. In a more recent moment of time there were those who were positive that the sun was God. They too were at best reluctant to relinquish so precious a tenet of faith.

The point to be made here is twofold. First: that throughout the course of man's restless quest for meaning in life the forms in which he thought he perceived that meaning changed as his knowledge of the universe expanded. And second: each such change was greeted with intense opposition.

Let us not pass too quickly or casually over the intercon-

nection between the enlargement of knowledge in general
and the view of God held at a particular point in time. Before
men knew that the changes of season are caused by immutable and automatic patterns of nature, it was easy—even
inevitable—that they be attributed to the immediate intervention of the gods. It therefore became incumbent upon
such men, as the days became perceptibly and alarmingly
shorter, to kindle huge fires of propitiation, that their gods
might be persuaded to take action toward reversing the
process and lengthening the duration of the days. Once it
became common knowledge that the days would in any
event begin to lengthen, without any direct intervention by
the gods, the possession of that knowledge necessarily
changed man's concept of deity as well as his patterns of
ritual. He may have continued kindling fires as winter's
solstice approached but the original reason was forgotten
and they were now rationalized as Chanukah candles or
Christmas lights. In short, growing knowledge has always
meant changing concepts of God.

If men were all equally intelligent or their ability to
assimilate new experience and thought were the same, religious progress could be measured in neat and comfortable
compartments. Obviously, however, this is not so. The result
is tension and strain between those who are restless to press
forward toward the future and those who are reluctant to
depart from the past. Hence the controversy in every age
between conservatives and liberals even within the same religious tradition. Hence the suspicion and fear with which
the majority in each age looks upon the spiritual innovations of the minority. Religious change—like any other
important kind of change—is always initiated by the few
and resisted by the many.

Moses Maimonides, Jewish philosopher, physician and
theologian of the twelfth century, is looked upon today by
all Jews as one of the most authentic spokesmen of traditional Judaism. In his own time he was a firebrand of con-

troversy. His assertions that God is pure spirit, that it is impossible to describe or define Him, that those who anticipate a physical heaven are like children demanding their reward of candy, were so scandalous to many of his contemporaries that his books were publicly burned. The religious conservatives within Judaism today are as apt to praise and quote him as were their psychological progenitors to accuse him of heresy.

All this has its ineluctable implications for today. If it be true that expanding knowledge leads to changing concepts of God, then our age above all others must expect such change. Never before has man's knowledge of the universe increased at so prodigious a pace. Maimonides found it necessary to reinterpret the idea of God within the framework of Aristotelian philosophy which was on the growing edge of learning in his time. We today must re-think our ideas of God in a context which includes the biological discoveries of Darwin, the physical insights of Einstein and the psychological imperatives of Freud. It has been estimated that man's knowledge of his universe may now be expected to double in each period of fifteen years. Any attempt to insulate religion from the swiftness of change in other areas of human experience dooms religion to sterility.

The fact that this truth is self-evident should not induce us to assume, however, that new concepts of God will be resisted any less bitterly today than in the past. Nor have we the right to look with scorn on those who have made so extensive an emotional investment in the old that they cannot risk involvement with the new, even though their interpretation of God may long since have ceased to function in any way other than providing them with a kind of comfortable emotional security. Our need is for men and women who, without rejecting those who neither understand nor accept their thinking, will nonetheless press forward persistently and courageously toward the future.

2

Though All Else Change

Through all their varying and evolving ways of groping for God, men were trying to express certain eternally important truths about their universe and themselves. On different levels of sophistication there may not be as much difference as we are at first tempted to assume between what the most primitive and the most modern of them were saying. If we can succeed now in extracting kernels of common truth from the outer and incidental husks of expression, we shall then be in a position to inquire (a) whether these kernels are still valid for ourselves and (b) if so, how they can be most meaningfully articulated for today.

In making this attempt perhaps it would be well temporarily to dispense with the word *God*. So many of us mean such widely divergent things when we use this word and some of us surround it, consciously or unconsciously, with such complicated emotional overtones, that the word may at this point confuse more than it clarifies. So, avoiding the language of theology as far as possible, let us ask ourselves: what were the generations of men, early and late, striving to say when they proclaimed their belief in God?

1. Our universe is characterized by law and order, by purpose and plan. Even primitive man was quickly convinced that his larger physical environment was too wondrous a setting to be the consequence only of coincidence and chance. The regular succession of seasons, the predictable timetable of sun and tide, the immutable operation of gravity—these and innumerable others among nature's patterns led him to conclude at a very early stage of his experience that his universe was not one of randomness or caprice.

2. Man is himself part of this cosmic plan, whatever it may be. He is not a detached observer looking on from outside. The plan operates through him. His little life takes on significance and meaning precisely insofar as it partakes of the larger and more important whole.

3. There is more to man than meets the eye. Which means to say: he is not just a physical being. Though he is, to be sure, a physical animal remarkably similar to other animals, though the laws of chemistry and physics assuredly operate within his body as they do elsewhere, he also possesses a conscience . . . a spirit . . . a mind . . . emotional proclivities, which no anatomist or surgeon will ever be able to identify in the form of a physical organ.

4. This is no less true of the universe than it is of man. Behind the physical phenomena of nature too there is a nonphysical or extraphysical reality. Religious men and women have never been able to describe this reality accurately or to know it fully but they were always convinced it existed.

5. Whatever man's part in the universal plan may be, it can be realized only through conscious and responsible action

by himself. He is not merely a passive vessel through which the plan flows and is automatically fulfilled. In the beginning man's responsibilities to the plan were understood largely in terms of ritual. Increasingly as he developed they were re-interpreted as ethical obligations. Always there were specific things man himself had to do, by the conscious exercise of his own will, in order for his potential as a participant in the larger plan to be realized.

6. When man does undertake this fulfillment of his individual obligation to the plan, there is something in the universe which helps him. He is not alone. His hopes are not doomed to total frustration. By the very nature of the universe and of himself, he can succeed. In his striving thus to succeed, moreover, rests his highest hope for happiness. Transient pleasure may be secured without regard to any cosmic plan or man's place in it. But long-range welfare and true happiness are dependent upon man's recognition of his role in the total scheme of things and his best effort to play this role well.

Here—admittedly in bare and inadequate outline, with argument and elaboration left for later—are the assumptions and convictions which men were struggling to understand and express whenever they affirmed their belief in God. And here is the valid test in our time too of whether or not one is religious. The man who believes that there is over-all purpose in the universe and in human life, that both nature and he himself consist of spiritual as well as physical reality, that he has an inescapable responsibility to conform to and promote the purposes of the universe, and that he is not abandoned or forlorn in undertaking this effort—such a man believes in God even if he verbally denies it. The man who asserts that he and nature are purely physical, mechanical accidents, that there is no purpose beyond what he may project for himself, that the universe is indifferent or antagonistic to his noblest aspirations—such a man denies God no matter how frequently or fervently he seems to call upon Him.

If the conclusions suggested above are no longer valid for our time, then we have outgrown not only the need but also the possibility of God. In that event, the sooner we acknowledge this fact, the better for us and the future. If, on the other hand, these hypotheses still square with reality, our primary religious responsibility is to find ways of expressing them which will be consistent with what we know about the universe. We have reached the point where it is necessary to test the authenticity for our time of those assumptions which religion has made for centuries. Before probing in that direction, however, a brief digression may be helpful.

▼ The Uses of Religion

At first it may seem crass to talk about religion in utilitarian terms. The fact is, however, that religion, like every other successful human invention or institution, has survived precisely because it has more or less effectively met certain human needs. While testing the tenability of religion for our time, then, let us keep in mind the proper role of religion in human experience, the purposes it may reasonably be expected to serve.

An inquiry of this nature assumes added importance from the widespread currency of two shabby misconceptions about the purpose of religion. One is the assumption that religious faith is a gilt-edged investment, guaranteed to pay profitable financial dividends. The following excerpts, culled from an ad published some years ago in New York newspapers, speak for themselves:

I talked with God . . . and as a result of that little talk with God a strange Power came into my life. After forty-two years of horrible, dismal, sickening failure, everything took on a brighter hue. . . . And now?—well, I am President of the News Review Publishing Company, which corporation publishes the largest circulating afternoon daily in North Idaho. I own the largest office building in my city. I drive two beautiful cars. I own my own home, which has a lovely pipe organ in it, and my family are abundantly provided for after I'm gone. And all this has been made possible because one day about twelve years ago I actually and literally talked with God. You too may experience that strange mystical Power which comes from talking with God.

We could afford to laugh at this sort of thing were it not for the frequency with which it is still seriously exploited. The acceptance and practice of religion has been recommended by some of the most popular preachers in the contemporary pulpit as a device for selling everything from real estate to vacuum cleaners. Unless we recognize that true religion bears no relationship whatever to affluence or material success, we shall be hopelessly stymied in our search for meaning of any kind.

A second gross misunderstanding of religion is that it can or should protect us from all the painful infections and abrasions of life, that its proper role (to change the metaphor intentionally) is to provide a smoothly paved by-pass around life's intersections of suffering and sorrow. Nothing could be farther from truth.

There has been much misunderstanding of what my beloved predecessor and friend, Joshua Loth Liebman, meant by "peace of mind." He did not intend it to justify irresponsible complacency or passing the buck to God. He knew that the only peace acceptable to mature religion is that of a man knowing in his heart that today he came reasonably close to doing everything in his personal power toward meeting his ethical responsibilities and promising that tomorrow he will strive to do even a little better.

The Talmud, ancient repository of Jewish law and lore, tells us explicitly: "The righteous shall have no complacency of spirit [modern reading: peace of mind] even in the world to come."

Not very long ago our newspapers reported a protest voiced by certain secretaries in offices adjacent to the central police barracks in Capetown, South Africa. These are the barracks in which beatings were administered to colored prisoners. It seems that their agonized cries made it impossible to concentrate on office work. One woman said: "I sympathize with the police. It cannot be nice to have to deal out these beatings. But I wish we didn't have to listen to it." The Capetown police were sufficiently impressed to shift future beatings to the basement of the building. Too much of what presumes to call itself religion today is like this protest: concerned not with the elimination of injustice, not with our personal involvement in establishing righteousness, but with muffling the sounds of anguish in order not to distract us from our accustomed ways. This, clearly and unmistakably, is not the way of real religion.

Then what is? Four affirmatives are almost implied in the foregoing negatives. First, religion should help us understand the significance and purpose of our lives. Science seeks to answer questions beginning with *what* and *how*. It leaves to philosophy and religion those which start with *why*. Man is fortunate in possessing an insatiable curiosity to answer both types of questions. He can never rest satisfied without the assurance that his brief span of earthly experience is of greater consequence than that of the ant, which goes diligently about its accustomed business until a sudden footstep from above crushes it into utter oblivion.

A second function of religion is to help us over the rough spots of life. No man can expect to escape all tragedy or sorrow. We need—all of us—shock absorbers to help us take those bumps which are unavoidable. We have a right to expect that religion will serve us in this way.

Third and even more importantly, religion should and must spur us on to higher standards of conduct. This is the truest touchstone of all. Later we shall see that religion and ethics are by no means synonymous. But ethical behavior is an essential ingredient of any religion worth the name. For myself, I have one question above all others to ask about any person's theology: "How does he behave differently because of his belief from the way he would without it?" Unless the difference in conduct is appreciable, it matters little indeed to me whether he believes or in what.

The fourth proper use of religion is in part at least a rephrasing of the third. It should function in each man's life as a catalyst, releasing and energizing his own highest and noblest potentialities. Few of us come anywhere near the fulfillment of our true capacities. Most of the time we are like motors, meant to produce enormous power, throbbing with impressive noise but yielding little energy because our gears are disengaged. Every one of us possesses the potential for more ethical action, for deeper sensitivity, for more creative expression, for richer love than we have ever realized. Religion and psychiatry—each by its own insights, each in its unique and special way—should enable us to fulfill a little more each day what we have it in us to become.

Rabbi Samuel Glasner comes very close to my understanding of religion's proper role in life when he suggests that its function is to direct us toward answering two questions: Who am I? And: What am I doing here?* Gordon Allport aims in the same direction when he writes: "A man's religion is . . . his ultimate attempt to enlarge and to complete his own personality by finding the supreme context

* From a paper read at the tenth meeting of the Committee for the Scientific Study of Religion, April 16, 1955

in which he rightly belongs."* Both of them would agree, I am sure, that consequent upon discovering the answers to these questions in words must come action, which is the best answer of all.

Where, then, do we stand? We have lamented the degree to which religion fails to function in our lives today. We have observed how man's concepts of God have constantly changed, yet have always struggled to articulate certain unchanging truths. And we have paused to inquire into the purposes which religion may be expected to serve. Now let us turn back again to those affirmations concerning the universe and life which faith in God has always symbolized. Are they still valid for the space age? Or do they voice an orientation to reality which is no longer tenable?

* *The Individual and His Religion,* The Macmillan Company, 1950, p. 142

3

Long Ladder of Life

More than a century ago the French philosopher Auguste Comte wrote: "When science has done its complete work, it will conduct God to the boundary of the universe and bow him out with thanks for His provisional services." This continues to be the opinion of those who believe that religion marked a stage in the growth of man from which we are about to emerge. I remember a college professor of mine who drew a neat diagram on his blackboard to represent this point of view. It consisted of a circle divided into two fairly equal halves. One was labeled *Known*, the other *Unknown*. Religion, we were told, deals with the latter, science with the former. The line of separation is a moving one. As man's knowledge is enlarged, the area of the *known* increases while that of the *unknown* is diminished. Thus, our professor impressed upon us, the province of religion is an inevitably contracting one which is destined one day to vanish altogether.

At the risk of prematurely anticipating a later argument, let it be hastily observed here that two fallacies marred the effectiveness of this diagram. For one thing it is simply not true that science limits itself to the *known* while religion deals only with the *unknown*. The whole thrust of science —especially of pure as distinguished from applied science— is to explore the *unknown*. And no religion which is not appreciably based on and derived from the *known* can long be tenable for modern man.

It is foolish, moreover, to assume that enlargement of the *known* leads to a proportionate diminution of the *unknown*. In a very real sense, the more we know, the more we realize how much we don't know. We today—precisely because we possess so many kinds of knowledge unavailable to our ancestors—are faced with ever so many more questions and doubts than they. On two counts, then, my professor's diagram was a misrepresentation of fact. But he has scarcely been the only one to view religion and science in terms of contradiction.

Not long after the Russians had successfully launched their first man-made satellite, one of their scientists issued a public statement intended as an obituary for God. He said that since Sputnik had penetrated far beyond the limits of heaven without encountering either angels or God, this proved conclusively that neither existed!

This might seem to settle the matter were it not for the fact that scientists at least as skilled as the Russian and philosophers no less sophisticated than Comte have arrived at quite different conclusions. Far from ushering the real meaning of God out of the universe or of men's minds, science in many ways seems to establish the universe as a far more wondrous pattern of law and order than our ancestors could ever have suspected it to be. Take, for example, the primary unit of organic life, the cell. One scientist, a biochemist, has written: "What is a cell? For many years it was thought to be a bag of jelly-like substance in which floated several bodies, notably the nucleus. Today we know it as a beautifully structured thing, made up of various bodies, of canals and vesicles, of small particles and amorphous material, all arranged and organized as if there were a definite reason for their existence and their placement."*

One of our nation's outstanding botanists, Dr. Edmund Sinnott, former Dean of the Graduate School at Yale University, calls our attention to a number of instances in which nature seems to be operating almost with the equivalent of conscious purpose. He uses the white pine tree as an example. Normally, the branches of such a tree grow in clusters around a "leader." While this "leader" grows straight upward toward the sky, the branches spread out from it at an angle of about seventy degrees from the trunk. Dr. Sinnott reports that if an entire cluster is bound together so that the offshoots are forced to grow straight with their "leader," the branches above the confining twine spread out at an angle to their own lower section in order to resume their original direction of growth.

In another experiment the "leader" was forced from its normally vertical position and tied at right angles to the trunk. Where it might be assumed that it would then continue to grow in that direction, such is not the case at all. Its growing tip swings back upward again, pointing once more toward the sky. I myself have seen how, when a "leader" has been destroyed, one of its branches takes over, as it were, to become a new "leader" for the cluster. Almost like a sergeant assuming command of his platoon when the lieutenant has been killed.

We are only on the threshold of understanding why such

* Philip Siekevitz, in *The Nation*, September 13, 1958

actions occur. There is reason to believe that phototropism —the attraction of living cells toward light—and the effect of gravity on the development of cells may have much to do with this sort of thing. Or—as Dr. Sinnott himself believes—there may be a principle of purposiveness within the organism and cell which persistently expresses itself. That we are not yet altogether able to explain such phenomena is not of immediate importance. That they develop as they do is impressive evidence that science confirms rather than destroys our picture of law and order in the universe.

I am aware of the fact that scientists no longer speak as they once did in terms of nature's *laws*. Today they speak instead of *statistical probability*. The distinction is more one of semantics than of substance. What it boils down to in oversimplified essence is that though the sun has appeared each day without exception over the eastern horizon and disappeared at night in the west, we cannot in technical truth prove that it will always be thus. All we can say with certainty is that so far as human memory and experience go, the sun has always acted this way in the past and the *statistical probability* is that it will continue so in the future. It is clear—is it not?—that what the strictly technical scientist here calls *probability* is precisely what we mean in ordinary language by the term *law*.

All we have a right and duty to expect of ourselves as modern men is that our philosophy or religion should explain the facts of universal life insofar as we know them. No explanation can provide in advance for all possible or imaginary eventualities. If at some future moment the sun should suddenly depart from the pattern it has thus far followed, then, to be sure, our philosophy would need refurbishing to take account of so portentous an event. In the meantime, the sun acts unexceptionally whether we call it probability or law. The more we learn through science, the more awesome and impressive the evidence becomes that this is indeed a universe of order.

Prominent scientists have said so explicitly. Thus Arthur Compton, Nobel Prize winner in physics: "The chance that a world such as ours should occur without intelligent design becomes more and more remote as we learn of its wonders."*
George Russell Harrison, Dean of the School of Science at the Massachusetts Institute of Technology, writes: "It is not difficult for a scientist to see the hand of God in the patterns which protons, neutrons and electrons take in forming atoms, and those which the atoms take to form molecules, molecules to form cells, cells to form tissues, organs, and bodies, and bodies to form social aggregates. . . . The basic tenets of all great religions, the distilled spiritual wisdom of humanity, coincides closely with what science reveals in nature. The universe is based on order, not on chaos and chance."†

▼ *Darwin Started It*

The most convincing evidence of all that science today confirms the first quintessential meaning of religion through the ages, comes from a careful study of evolution. This may seem surprising to those who recall how vigorously some religious groups resisted the idea of evolution. The wife of the Canon of Worcester Cathedral, when told of Darwin's theory, is reported to have exclaimed: "Descended from the apes! My dear, we hope it is not true. But if it is, let us pray that it may not become generally known."

Today it is true and generally known that man, if not quite literally descended from the apes, has evolved from

* *Man's Destiny in Eternity* (The Garvin Lectures), Beacon Press, 1949, p. 11
† *What Man May Be*, William Morrow and Company, 1956, pp. 229, 244.
© 1953, 1955, 1956, by George Russell Harrison

origins common to both. Evolution is no longer an uncon-
firmed hypothesis. From all the evidence available to us,
and at least until such unlikely time as contrary evidence of
greater weight is discovered, it appears to be fact that at
some point in the past, probably about two billion years
ago, in a manner which the wisest among us has scarcely
begun to understand, life made its first appearance on this
planet in the form of microscopic protogenes which emerged
in the primeval slime. And that every form of life known
since or now has developed from that first form.

Slow, imperceptible mutations in the cell led in the long
course of time to new species and breeds. In the beginning
there was only the individual cell. Then cells "learned" to
combine, to work together in multi-cellular organisms.
Protozoa begot water worms . . . water worms begot shell
fish and sponges . . . these begot fish with backbones . . .
fish with backbones begot amphibians . . . amphibians begot
reptiles, small and great; among these were the birds . . .
reptiles begot mammals, the highest and most ingenious of
which are human beings. The story is ever so much more
complicated and involved than these hasty phrases indicate.
Millions of mutations were the making of each apparently
simple change. Thousands of species and stages appeared for
each one listed above. Many of the life-forms which once
populated the earth have long since vanished. But the main
outline is clear. From the simplest, most mysterious of beginnings, life surged upward through the millennia from a
single cell to a man. The first creature that could, even by
a generous stretching of the imagination, be called human
probably appeared on earth about a million years ago. The
first that really resembled ourselves goes back no more than
perhaps two hundred fifty thousand years.

The facts are exposed for all to see. The explanation is
still obscure. No one knows, at least yet, how or why
the first protogenes appeared or what caused the successive

stages of development from that day to this. But men have speculated at length and it may add illumination to our inquiry if we pause at this point to consider one or two of their answers. In doing so let us bear in mind the two aspects in which the scientist may speak to us. When he charts the successive stages through which evolution has progressed—the *what* and *how* of evolution—he speaks as a scientist in the name of science. He deals then with fact to the extent that the disciplines he follows have enabled him to discover fact, and we ignore his conclusions at great peril to our own integrity and to the cause of truth.

But when the same scientist begins to speculate on the *why* of evolution—when he enters the realm of whether the whole breath-taking adventure is purely the consequence of chance or only a concomitant of bio-chemical reactions or also a response to in-dwelling purpose and power—then he speaks not as scientist but as man. He has crossed the line from science to philosophy. He is dealing not with fact alone but with the attempt to explain fact. No less than the scientifically oriented religionist engaged in the same effort, he is now articulating a faith toward which his examination of fact propels him. Here his standing as an expert may be no better, as indeed it is probably no worse, than that of the philosopher or religionist who possesses a profound respect for truth.

What, then, are some of the tentative answers already proposed for the riddle of evolution?

▼ *A Lucky Accident?*

To begin with, there are those—many scientists of repute among them—who believe the first appearance of life on this earth and the entire process of evolution which followed came about through sheer chance. In essence what they say is that, given a long enough period of time, a large enough assortment of chemical components and a wide enough variance in temperature and other conditions, it is entirely possible that somewhere along the line a living cell would appear by coincidence, with no purpose or plan operating either within itself or from the outside. The key to this line of thinking is the prodigious number of possibilities out of which such a chance event might emerge. What would seem to be beyond belief if we were dealing only with a few centuries or a small area of space assumes, we are told, a different dimension of possibility when millions of years are involved and an entire planet of chemical raw materials.

The reasoning here can be illustrated by the claim that if a large enough group of monkeys were trained to sit at typewriters, pounding their keys at random over a sufficiently long period of centuries, eventually one of them by sheer chance would succeed in typing out the Bible. In short, if the range of possibilities is made large enough and the span of time sufficiently protracted, anything could happen by coincidence.

A considerable number of laboratory experiments have already been initiated in the hope that the conditions out of which organic life first emerged can be artificially reproduced and a protogene like the first one in time be synthetically created by man. Some scientists seem to feel they have already come close to the point of success in these experiments. Without indulging at this point in polemic or debate, it should be noted at once that even if they succeed, they will not have proved by any means the accidental origin of life. For at best what they will have accomplished is the creation of life through the application of purpose and intelligence to the raw materials involved. This would amount to a duplication, under conditions of stringent laboratory control, of that which occurred aeons ago without benefit of such aids.

Those who believe that the very first form of life appeared in this purely coincidental way would then go on to assert that each subsequent mutation took place in the same way, that all evolution is explicable as the chance reactions of chemical and physical processes on one another. They might also introduce the possibility of natural selection, which we shall consider in a moment.

No one can prove in any definitive way that the proponents of such theories are wrong—any more than they can prove themselves to be right. We are a long way yet from any such certainty of knowledge. What we can do, however, is examine their ideas in the light of our best logic and experience, including that which emanates from science itself. Consequent upon precisely such an examination, Professor Edwin Conklin, eminent Princeton University biologist, concluded: "The probability of life originating from accident is comparable to the probability of the Unabridged Dictionary resulting from an explosion in a printing factory."

We must bear in mind, moreover, that even after getting over the hump of the first protogenes, there is more by far to be accounted for in subsequent developments. In order for life to develop in anything like the manner we know, there were billions upon billions of crucial junctures at which the right development had to take place in the right way and at the right time. It is as if there were a train traveling over many billions of miles of track toward a given destination. Spaced only yards apart are switches beyond counting, each of which must be set accurately for the destination to be reached. Shall we assume, then, that the goal can be reached just by leaving the setting of each switch to chance?

There is an obvious rejoinder at this point. How do we know that if the switches had been set differently, the train would not have reached another equally desirable destination? The implication of which is: if biological developments other than those which actually occurred had taken place at the critical junctures already mentioned, is it not possible that some other form of life would have resulted? In strict honesty our answer must be affirmative. Theoretically no one can prove that such would not have been the case. But here again our task is to explain, if we can, the facts of life *as we know them*, not as we may imagine they could have been. And the only forms of life we know are those we see here.

Dr. Harlow Shapley, one-time Director of the Harvard Observatory, has postulated a high probability that life of some sort exists on other planets as well as our own. When and if his theory is confirmed, one of two possibilities will eventuate. Either (a) the best explanations, scientific and philosophic, which the human mind has been able to achieve on this earth to account for what we have experienced here will prove to be broad and valid enough to encompass the new phenomena also—or (b) the new data will disprove what we now believe to be true, in which case we shall have to push the frontiers of our philosophic exploration still further. But remember: all this deals with a theoretical possibility which may never exist in fact. That life exists in particular forms on this planet now is not theory; it is fact. That the evolutionary process has led from simplest beginnings, through incredibly complicated way-stations, to human intelligence and spirit, we know to be true. The task before us, then, is to determine, if we can, whether that which we know to be fact seems likely to have resulted from a combination of coincidence and chance.

For myself, to believe that the vast multitude of developments and changes necessary for evolution to have reached its present position could have been entirely accidental is to accept on faith miracles far beyond any reported in the Bible. It would be far easier for me to believe—as I do not—that the Red Sea literally split before Moses or that the whale swallowed Jonah (or for that matter even that Jonah swallowed the whale) than to believe that the path from protogene to Albert Einstein was a colossal cosmic accident.

There are eminent scientists who seem to agree. Julian Huxley, world-renowned biologist, has tried to compute mathematically the odds against a horse developing from the earliest form of life by chance mutations. I don't pretend to understand his method. Nor can I fully grasp the enormity of his solution when he announces the odds as 1 out of 1,000 multiplied to the millionth power, which is the same as saying 1 followed by 3,000,000 zeroes! It would take three large volumes of about five hundred pages each just to write that figure down. And this carries evolution only up to the horse, with its most exhilarating accomplishments still ahead!*

I am much more impressed by Huxley's mathematics than by what seems to me his altogether contradictory conclusion that despite this evidence the horse did indeed develop by a combination of chance mutations and natural selection. For me, Huxley's figures are far less consistent with his own conclusion than with that of physician and bio-chemist William S. Beck: "When one reflects on the stupendous complexity of the living organism, it is entirely reasonable to doubt that it could have arisen as the result of a chance event completely physical in character."†

▼ *The Road to Survival?*

We have already observed that some of those who would explain evolution partly on the basis of chance would also incorporate natural selection in their explanation. In my own college days this was assumed to be the whole answer to

Evolution in Action, Harper & Brothers, 1953, p. 46
† *Modern Science and the Nature of Life*, Harcourt, Brace and Company, 1957, p. 242

the mystery of evolution. We were taught that from the vast number of mutations which occurred through the millennia by chance, only those persisted which had survival value, which adapted their possessors to the environment in a superior way.

Let us assume, for example, that at a certain moment in the career of a given species, through a series of mutations occurring by chance, some individuals began to develop longer and stronger legs. These individuals would then presumably have been able to run faster than others and thus more effectively to escape or avoid danger. In the course of time those with short legs who were slower of speed would succumb to enemies from whom they had been unable to escape. They would therefore have less opportunity to propagate. Those with longer legs and faster speed and hence greater likelihood of survival would also be the ones able to reproduce themselves and to pass on to their progeny the mutations which had led to their longer legs. Thus, in an extended period of centuries, a change would develop in that particular species, a change altogether accountable in terms of natural selection through adaptation to environment.

We need not limit ourselves to such hypothetical examples. At an earlier stage of the earth's existence its entire surface was apparently covered with water. It was at such a time that the first single-celled organisms appeared. They were able to obtain from their environment the oxygen essential to life only by extracting it from the water in which they lived. Slowly, however, the water receded from large areas of the earth's surface. Those organisms which were adaptable to the new kind of environment, which through countless mutations had developed a capacity to obtain their oxygen directly from the earth's atmosphere rather than through water, were able, by surviving on dry land, to reproduce and refine in their offspring precisely the innovations they had been the first to develop themselves. Those, on the other hand, which possessed only the old adaptive equipment were doomed either to perish or to remain in the water, where they promptly formed a dead-end in evolution.

There can be no doubt that natural selection has indeed played a large and important role in the development of life. Yet there are several considerations which caution us not to assume that this is anything like the complete explanation. For one thing, if adaptation to environment were the principal motivation of evolution, the entire process could have ended long ago. Biologically speaking, certain kinds of worms are far better adapted to the environment than are men. They achieved a highly successful adaptation something like six hundred million years ago and haven't changed since. Every level of evolutionary development beyond theirs would seem to indicate that something more is operating here than mere adaptation.

Indeed, some of the most important changes which occurred after the worm stage were anything but successful attempts to cope with the environment. At least in their beginnings they made survival more precarious rather than more certain. At the time, for example, when the first rather fragile mammals began to appear, the dominant reptiles were ever so much better adapted to the prevailing environment than were these biological innovations. Based on everything known up to that time, the odds would certainly have seemed overwhelming on survival of the reptiles rather than the newly emerging mammals. Yet we know that ultimately the reptiles were by-passed while mammals became "the wave of the future." Can adaptation alone help us account for that?

We have already referred to the development of lungs which enabled life to survive on dry land. There is grave danger that in retrospect we may telescope the development of centuries into moments and establish in our minds a sequence of events which simply didn't exist. Actually the changes which would ultimately be necessary if life were to adapt itself to dry land began to appear many thousands of years before they were needed. Otherwise there would never have been time for them to be consummated as successful adaptations, for such changes occur with painful slowness. At a time long before the drying off of the waters, two significant changes had already begun to develop in certain species of fish. One was the development of extra size and strength in fins on the bottom side of the body. The other was the development of a swim-bladder inside the body. Neither was necessary as an adaptation to environment when it first appeared. Yet both proved imperative at a later time. For the exaggerated fin was the beginning of the leg and the strong swim-bladder eventually developed into the lung. When the waters began to diminish, those fish which had thus "experimented" biologically thousands of years before, perhaps even at some risk to their survival then, proved to be the very ones able to move from one pond or lake to another and thus to be the vehicles for further advance in evolution! The Canadian zoölogist, N. J. Berrill, puts it this way: "In a general way fish were forced into fitness for living out of water before either need or opportunity really arose."*

What all this adds up to is that some of the most important adaptations we know took place, not as adaptations to existing environment but in anticipation, as it were, of future environment! As if life itself somehow seemed to know that a particular change had to be prepared in advance for a later moment of need! William Howells, a leading American anthropologist, may have had this very kind of thing in mind when he wrote: "Evolution is not so simple as that, and natural selection, which once bore all before it, is no longer

* *You and the Universe*, Dodd, Mead and Company, 1958, p. 106

accepted by naturalists generally as the only key, or even the main one."*

This chapter must not be construed as ruling out chance and adaptation altogether. Within the limited number of possibilities allowed by nature's laws, chance in all likelihood played a role. We have already observed the importance of adaptation or natural selection as an instrument of the evolutionary process. Our claim here is not that chance and adaptation are nonexistent, but that not even the two of them together, pushed to the farthest extremes of probability, suffice to explain the whole of evolution. Something more is needed.

A final word on the subject of chance: Often we ascribe a given phenomenon to chance simply because we are as yet unable exactly to identify or assess the laws by which it is governed. For example: when throwing dice, we say that the final configuration after the cubes have come to rest is a matter of chance. Actually, it isn't that at all. If one could compute every factor involved in a specific instance of throwing dice—their position in the hand at the outset, the exact direction and strength of the thrust, the weight and balance of the cubes themselves, the composition and slope of the surface on which they are being thrown, etc., etc.—it would be found that the dice perform strictly according to law. One who knew in advance every factor involved should in theory be able to predict the end-result of each throw. The word *chance* is here a cover-up for our ignorance, not an accurate description of what takes place. In like manner, it may be that a part at least of what we are now inclined to ascribe to chance in the development of evolution will one day be understood as quite the contrary of real chance.

As we reach the human level of evolution, the inadequacy of natural selection as a total explanation becomes even

* *Mankind So Far*, Doubleday, Doran and Company, 1945, pp. 7 f.

more apparent. What, for example, is the survival value of music? Or the enjoyment and pursuit of beauty? Or the writing of poetry? Of what possible adaptive value could primitive man's efforts have been when he first began to scratch crude drawings on the walls of his cave? Yet all these are obviously chapters in the exhilarating story of evolution, chapters beyond explanation as a combination of chance and adaptation to environment. Our search for meaning in evolution will have to continue.

4

Where Are We Headed?

As we look back across the millennia of evolutionary development on this earth, are there any discernible directions? Or does the whole process seem to have unfolded at random? When one examines steel filings carelessly scattered on a flat surface, no pattern or design is apt to be apparent. If a magnet has been applied to such filings, however, its organizing effect can be traced at once even by one who first comes upon the scene and is unaware of what has happened. Are there any traces of direction or design in the multitudinous mutations which have made evolution possible?

Some scientists of repute—among them so eminent an authority as George Gaylord Simpson, Chairman of the Department of Geology and Paleontology in the American Museum of Natural History—deny that there is any plan in evolution. They give as a substantial reason the fact that whatever progress man can trace in evolution has not been unbroken. There have been many biological experiments which failed, many detours and dead-ends. While it is true that some mutations have caused the progression from protogene to man, others have led to the total extinction of some species along the way. If there were plan, they say, the line of progression would be straight and uninterrupted.

What appears at this point to be a major disagreement is, I suspect, more a matter of semantics than of substance. If the word *plan* is conceived in terms of an architect laying out specifications for a house—with every last detail ineluctably plotted before the first shovel of earth is turned—evolution admittedly was not planned. I do not believe that God knew in advance every form or stage life would assume in its upward thrust from protogene to man.

But is there not another legitimate meaning to the word *plan?* Unlike that of the architect, imposed in advance from without, is there not also a kind of plan which proceeds on its own momentum from within? Like that which unfolds when a rosebush develops from a seed or an oak tree from an acorn. The new bush will not be a precise replica of the one from which the seed came. Nor can its exact description or size be anticipated. These attributes depend not only on the pattern or plan inherent in the seed, but also on such environmental factors as climate and soil. Identical seeds (if there were such) planted, one in a barren desert, the other in rich loam, would produce vastly different bushes.

The fact that the process of growth is not totally detailed or predestined from the beginning does not negate the presence of pattern or plan. The fact is that—given the conditions prerequisite for growth—the seed will always develop into a rosebush, never into anything else. Shoots and leaves and thorns will always precede buds; buds will always precede blossoms; blossoms will always, after a time, wither and fade. There is inherent, in-dwelling plan—subject, of course, to change by outer circumstance. But no natural outer circumstance can so alter the innate plan as to transform the "intention" of the rose seed into the blossom of a tulip.

In short, the word *plan* is used here to designate (a) the existence of laws in conformity with which (b) a given organism can develop only in directions consistent with its own nature. This is fairly clear with regard to a specific organism or species. What we want to discover in this chapter is whether any such plan can be found in the evolutionary process as such.

The evidence given by those who deny any plan in evolution may be such as to disprove God's acting from outside the process to implement, step by step, a design all laid out and anticipated by Him from the beginning. It does not eliminate the possibility of plan in terms of general directions, acting as a ferment from within the process itself. It is this second kind of plan for which we shall now search. It doesn't require that the exact forms to be assumed by life were foreseen or predestined from the beginning—only that certain major directions were implicit in the process from its start and that adaptation or natural selection was the instrument which progressively determined the specific forms through which these directions were to work themselves out.

An analogy may help. The law of gravity is an example of plan inherent within the universe. On this earth that law manifests itself, among other ways, in the fact that water will always flow downhill. If a spring breaks through the surface of the earth near the top of a mountain, the precise course of flow to be followed by its stream is not foreordained. What is clearly predestined is that the water will flow downward, its path to be influenced by the contours of the land and the position of such obstacles as rocks. In short, the inherent principle or plan will direct the water; adaptation to existing circumstances will determine the precise course of its path. In much the same manner it is possible to find in evolution the larger directions which indicate purpose and plan. The specific vessels through which the plan has thus far fulfilled itself have indubitably been molded in part by the instrument of adaptation.

In looking now for direction in evolution, we must not anticipate too much in the way of immediate or irrefutable result. Man has inhabited our earth only a tiny fraction of the time earth has existed and his awareness of the evolutionary process occupies less than a fraction of a fraction. Yet even this fleeting instant enables us, I believe, to find tracings of direction which may be our most powerful aid in the search for meaning.

The first such direction is that of organization and order. There is little evidence of order in the behavior of the individual molecule. It moves about at random in a manner which is entirely unpredictable. If, for example, a given quantity of solution B, which is blue, is poured into a container of solution W, which is white, it is impossible to predict the direction of movement which will be taken by any individual molecule of the blue substance. Its behavior, once poured, is altogether unpredictable and fortuitous. In theory at least, all the molecules of B could move to the right, separating the merged fluid into a blue half on the right and a white half on the left, with no physical partition between them. In practice—assuming the two liquids to be of equal density—this never happens. In practice the invading molecules of blue will always distribute themselves equitably—just as many moving to the right as to the left, upward as downward—giving us a fluid of common and constant color throughout. In short, while the movement of each molecule by itself is unpredictable, the movement of many molecules combined is orderly.

The purposive order thus inherent in evolution from its beginnings becomes more impressive when the molecules are components of living cells rather than of inert matter. Recent experiments at the Rockefeller Institute illustrate this dramatically. Such organs as kidneys and livers were extracted from the embryos of chickens at stages ranging from one-third to two-thirds of their normal period of development. The cells in these organs were then separated from each other and scrambled. Individual cells of a given organ—split from each other, divorced from their host organ and its larger organism—were then transplanted to the membrane of another chick embryo which could provide them with nourishment and blood. When these cultures were allowed to develop, microscopic studies disclosed that the extracted cells had grown together again to form functioning organs—kidneys or livers as the case may be. They had "refused" to be diverted from the direction of development apparently inherent in their original status.

Just how many molecules must be joined together or how many cells of the same kind must be combined for disorder to yield to order, we do not yet know. That there is a stage at which this occurs, however, becomes increasingly evident. We must not press the point too far. Edmund Sinnott is convinced that even in the tiniest primordial forms of life there is a *principle of organicism* out of which ultimately the human spirit and mind emerge. He would perhaps not agree then that at one stage there is no evidence of order at all but would assert instead that order or at least the potential toward order has been present, though not evident, from the beginning. I think he would not quarrel, however, with our conclusion that in either event the higher one goes on the ladder of life, the more evident do organization and order become. This will become clearer as we turn to a second direction in evolution, one closely related to this first.

▼ *Where Love Begins*

It is the direction of cooperation. Much has been made of the cruel competitiveness of nature . . . perhaps too much. To deny that nature in the raw is often calloused and cruel would be irresponsibly naïve. But it is no less irreverent of fact to overlook the immense importance of cooperation in nature's scheme of things or to forget that the whole adventure of evolution is dependent upon cooperation. This becomes self-evident when two hitherto independent cells "learn" to live together. Prior to that magic moment each single-celled organism had to perform every biological function for itself: digestion, motion, reproduction, elimination —all had to be provided by one and the same single cell. When two, then four, then eight, then sixteen cells "discovered" how to combine and remain together in one organism, they also began the process of specialization and cooperation. Which means to say, one group of cells undertook the function of digestion not only for themselves but for the entire organism. At the same time another group assumed the job of motion for all, another the task of reproduction for all, and so on and on.

Cells thus became dependent upon one another. Their very survival demanded cooperation. Without such cooperation neither survival nor the further development of evolution would have been possible. It would not be stretching the facts too much at all to suggest that here, in these first forms of life consisting of many cells, was the biological basis for what later, on the human level, became love.

If it is scarcely recognizable as such, this is because an enormous stretch of time and multitudinous stages of development intervene between beginning and consummation. But the direction, once established, is discernible throughout. We see it in the difference between parasitism and symbiosis.

There is an element of competition, at times even of cruelty, in the former. The flea living on the dog is a parasite. It cannot live without the dog or an equivalent host. It takes from the dog and gives nothing back in return except discomfort and annoyance. The bacteria in the human intestine, however, are in quite a different category. The bacteria, to be sure, cannot live without the nourishment obtained from me. But by the same token neither can I live without them. My ability to digest food and convert it into needed energy depends upon them. Thus we need each other. This is symbiosis. The biologically technical term must not obscure the fact that it represents cooperation and mutual interdependence and that, later in evolution, these qualities become love.

The higher one goes in tracing the course of evolution, the truer does it appear that the individual cell derives its importance not merely from its own existence as such but from its contribution to the on-going life of the larger organism of which it forms a part. This is true even in terms of longevity. The atoms in our bodies possess a shorter life span than the cells; the cells live more briefly than the body as a whole. It has been established that fewer than two percent of the atoms present in a human body at any point in time were in that body a year before. Each second in the life of a normal, healthy human being three million of his red blood cells die and are simultaneously replaced by an equal number of new ones. The lifetime of a given red blood cell is four months.

Which means to say that within the last year virtually every atom in my body has been replaced once and every red blood cell three times. The same is true of other cells within me, though the rate of replacement may be slower. Whenever an atom or cell dies, its place is taken at once by another which assumes the same function toward maintaining my life and health. Nature has assigned a much higher priority to the survival and development of the plant or animal or human organism as a whole than to any of their constituent atoms or cells. Healthy biological cells cooperate for the greater purpose of preserving the organism to which they belong.

The cell which refuses to be bound by this higher purpose is cancerous. Cancer is essentially a group of cells which has rejected, so to speak, the ordinary discipline of nature, which refuses to cooperate for the greater good of the whole body, which persists in accelerating its own growth at a rate that jeopardizes the body's survival. Unless successfully arrested, such cells soon commit suicide themselves by murdering the body as a whole. Dr. Boris Sokoloff, a physician and research scientist who has written extensively on the subject of cancer, tells us: "The most striking characteristic of cancerous tissue is its low social morale, as it were. Cancer cells disregard the interests of the organism as such, they do not care any longer for cellular organization. . . . A few cells, or a group of cells, originally normal and healthy, assert their freedom from the regulating forces of the organism. They begin to live an independent existence."*

One distinguished scientist presses the point even further than I have here. Pierre Teilhard de Chardin, brilliant paleontologist and priest, locates the first appearance of cooperation in nature even earlier than the symbiotic relationship among separate cells. He writes: "First the molecules of carbon compounds with their thousands of atoms symmetrically grouped, next the cell which, at the very smallest, contains thousands of molecules linked in a complicated system; then the metazoa in which the cell is no more than an almost infinitesimal element; and later the

---

*From *Science and the Purpose of Life*, by Boris Sokoloff, pp. 90, 105. Copyright, © 1950, by Boris Sokoloff. Used by permission of Farrar, Straus & Cudahy, Inc.

manifold attempts made by the metazoa to enter into symbiosis and raise themselves to a higher biological condition." And later: "If there were no *internal propensity to unite*, even at a prodigiously rudimentary level—indeed in the molecule itself—it would be physically impossible for love to appear higher up . . ."* (emphasis added).

Without denying for a moment, then, that competition—sometimes relentless and fierce—has characterized the processes of nature, it is important to remember that cooperation has been no less indigenous and essential to life's upward thrust.

Without symbiosis—which means to say, without cooperation—evolution would have been arrested very close to its beginnings. The role of cooperation increases, moreover, the higher we ascend the ladder of life. Atoms must "cooperate" in order for molecules to survive, molecules for the sake of cells, cells for the sake of organs, organs in order that organisms may develop and persist. Until finally we reach the stage of community, that is to say, the level on which organisms as such must live together or not at all.

Foreshadowings of community appear long before the development of man. The highly involved cooperation evident in ant society has often been utilized as an example. What is not so widely known is that the ant has two stomachs, one for itself and one for food to be shared with other ants.† Clearly, then, cooperation is a second direction in which the evolutionary process has been tending. It reaches its apex with the appearance of man. That element of competition which was essential to survival at an earlier and lower level becomes a threat on the human level. Here is the essential fallacy of those who attempt to justify war as an extension of the competition to be found in nature. There was a time, to be sure, when a certain amount of

* *The Phenomenon of Man*, Harper & Brothers, 1959, pp. 243 f., 264
† National Geographic Society, New York *Times*, January 4, 1961

"war" among species may have been nature's only way of maintaining a balance which would pave the way toward further and higher development of life. But on the human level of development that time is now past. We have reached the stage in evolution where that kind of competition can mean only extinction, where survival from this point on demands more and more cooperation.

A third direction discernible in evolution may sound inconsistent with the second. It is the direction of individualization. In the words of Dr. Boris Sokoloff, who has already added in this chapter to our understanding of cancer, "the evolution of individuality almost parallels the evolutionary processes of the living world."[*] Individualization too appears at a very early stage in the evolutionary process. We have already seen that evolution comes about through mutations. And mutations appear only in the cell which is different, which does not conform exactly to the norm, which dares, as it were, to be a unique individual. If each cell through eternity had been the exact replica of every other cell, there would never have been any such thing as evolution.

In another sense too, individualization appears at a very early point in the upward thrust of evolution. This is with respect to function. The process of cell specialization, already described, of necessity meant differentiation among the cells. If all remained exactly alike, all would be limited to the same general kind of functions. In that event the multicellular organism would gain over the single cell only in bulk, not in complexity, and evolution would have been arrested near its inception. Only as cells developed differences of function—which is another way of saying individualization—was evolution able to advance.

There is yet another way in which nature's propensity for individualization becomes apparent. This is in the profligate extravagance of her life forms. It has been estimated

[*] *Op. cit.* p. 82

that more than a million identifiable forms of plant, insect and animal life are extant on the earth today. No one knows the number that have already become extinct. Some biologists have denied any plan to evolution precisely because of this variety and divergence. They say that had there been any inherent plan, life would have evolved more efficiently and directly toward its goal. This is to assume that nature is as much in haste as her most complicated product seems to be.

N. J. Berrill, observing the phenomena of evolution from the perspective of an eminent scientist, says that it impresses him this way: "All as though an intelligent experimenter had the goal in mind but had to feel his way with the method."* The enormous variety of forms through which the life-force in nature has expressed itself does not of necessity negate the existence of plan; it simply indicates that in thrusting toward fulfillment of this plan, nature has operated by trial and error. It also demonstrates on a lavish scale that immense variety—which means to say, individualization—is an inherent direction of evolution.

No two blades of grass on all the earth are identical. No two peas—not even in the same pod—are precisely alike. What is true on so elementary a level as the single cell, the blade of grass or the pea is both truer and more significant in human life. No two men are exactly alike physically, not even so-called identical twins. In terms of personality the differences are even greater. Ancient Jewish wisdom, commenting on the Biblical story of creation, lauded God especially for the uniqueness of His individual human creatures. By way of analogy, it pointed to the fact that when a man makes many coins from a single mold, all are precisely alike. But God, who created all human beings in the same mold, was nonetheless able to make each one in some respects unique.

The apparent inconsistency between cooperation and in-

* *You and the Universe,* Dodd, Mead and Company, 1958, p. 145

dividualization as directions in evolution need not worry us. This is the kind of paradox which may at times defy logic but is amazingly true to fact. The cell which mutates as part of a larger organism becomes thereby a more significant "individual" than the isolationist cell which mutates alone. Its uniqueness is enhanced rather than impaired by the fact that it is circumscribed by a larger whole.

On the human level, where for the first time the word *individual* can really be written without quotation marks or qualification, the paradox is even more meaningful. A human being does not become truly a person except in relationship to other persons. The larger and more purposeful the social groupings within which he exists, so to speak, as a single cell, the greater the opportunity to develop his individual uniqueness. The more he is forced to turn in upon his own resources alone—which means to say, the less he exists as part of and responsive to such larger groupings—the less his chance to amplify his own uniqueness. You and I, living in community with our fellowmen, can individualize ourselves far more effectively than could Robinson Crusoe on his island.

The reciprocal relationship between the individual and the group is a delicate one. We have already observed how excessive "individualization" of the cell can destroy the organism by cancer. Preoccupation of the individual human organism with itself can wreak the same havoc on the group. Even so, inordinate emphasis on the group—the tribe, the sect, the cult, the nation—can destroy the individual. It is only when cooperation and individualization exist side by side—neither for itself alone, both for themselves and each other—that the potential of each can be fulfilled. Thus both are inherent directions of evolution.

▼ *From Rocks to Men*

A fourth direction is freedom. Again, there is an apparent inconsistency. Freedom may seem to contradict what has already been said about the randomness of the individual molecule contrasted to the orderliness of the larger aggregate. The contradiction, I think, is more apparent than real. There is a considerable difference between freedom and mere absence of predictability and order. True freedom demands an element of order. And true freedom is one of the directions in which evolution seems to be headed.

We see it as we examine certain objects typical of various evolutionary levels. Take, for example, the rock. What "freedom" does it have? Not even that of motion. To paraphrase Gertrude Stein: a rock is a rock is a rock. It is there, "free" to be moved by forces sufficient to counteract its own inertia, but really not free at all. A tree or flower is a higher stage of development than a rock. It also possesses a more substantial, though still severely limited, degree of freedom. It moves more frequently and easily. It can even reverse its "normal" direction of growth, as we saw in the case of the pine tree. It can enter into a symbiotic relationship with other forms of life, as a flower does with a bee. Clearly it has more freedom than a rock.

A dog is on yet a higher level of evolution than a tree or flower. It also shows still greater evidence of freedom. It is no longer rooted to one specific place. It moves about not only in response to force applied from the outside, but also as a result of force within itself. It possesses a certain amount of what may properly be called voluntarism. It represents, therefore, an expansion in life's capacity to be free.

Human beings, finally, are more highly developed than rocks or flowers or dogs. They also possess the greatest amount of freedom. They are free not only to move voluntarily but also to think speculatively, to create consciously and to discern the moral difference between good and evil. Later we shall examine the extent to which men possess free will. For the moment it will suffice to say that, whatever we mean by that term and to whatever extent the free will of man may be limited, undeniably he possesses and exhibits more of it than do the forms of life which preceded him on this planet. Hence, another direction in evolution is freedom.

A fifth and final direction is more difficult to label precisely. We spoke of it by inference in an earlier chapter when mentioning the non-material or extraphysical aspects of human life. It may truly be said that man is not only a higher *degree* of life than any other produced on this planet thus far but that he is also a different *kind* of life. Dr. Sinnott puts it this way: "Man . . . is so different from the beasts that he is another sort of being. Although he has clambered up the evolutionary stairway, he has in the process passed a critical point where he became not simply the highest form of life but a different creature from any of those that had preceded him."*

George Gaylord Simpson agrees. Comparing man to all previous forms of life, he writes of "an absolute difference in kind and not only a relative difference of degree." Later he adds: "It is still false to conclude that man is *nothing but* the highest animal or the most progressive product of organic evolution. He is also a fundamentally new sort of animal and one in which, although organic evolution continues on its way, a fundamentally new sort of evolution has also appeared."†

With the appearance of man, something new is injected

* Edmund W. Sinnott: *Matter, Mind and Man*, Harper & Brothers, 1957, p. 221
† *The Meaning of Evolution*, Yale University Press, 1949, pp. 284, 286

into the evolutionary process, something which has been ad-umbrated before, to be sure, but which appears in identifiable form for the first time now. Prior to man life developed purely on a physical level. The changes which appeared were entirely biological changes. It is not necessary to go all the way with Julian Huxley in asserting that from this point on in evolution further biological change will be negligible, to perceive that the most significant and meaningful kind of change will henceforth be spiritual. Which means to say, beginning with man evolution proceeds on both a physical and an extraphysical dimension and the most significant kind of development from now on will be the latter.

In speaking of man's spiritual development, we have refer-ence primarily to his conscience, his capacity to think and his conscious creativity. No earlier forms of life possessed these traits. Various kinds of animals can be trained to do certain things and to refrain from doing others purely on the basis of associating specific behavior patterns with either pleasure or pain; but none other than man can imaginatively evaluate a proposed new kind of act as being moral or im-moral. A dog can look pathetically regretful in anticipation of punishment but it cannot experience guilt. Harlow Shapley has described lying on his belly by the hour, observ-ing the behavior of ants. He tells of having thus seen amazing examples of cooperation and foresight, of mutual dependence and zeal. That these are related to similar characteristics in man, it would be nonsense to deny. To claim that they are identical or equal, however, would be no less preposterous. What the ant is able to do in a primitive way by unconscious instinct, man performs on an incomparably larger scale by conscious choice.

Other animals can reason to a certain extent, as the rat does in finding its way to food in a maze, but they are not able to speculate on the course of evolution or the meaning of life. When an animal lower than man happens to "create" something of beauty, like the glorious color of a blossom or the exquisite texture of a bird's nest, this is merely an incidental and automatic consequence of some instinctive pattern which is conducive to survival. At least as far as our planet is concerned, man—and only man—has evolved to the point of conscious and deliberate spirituality, another way of saying that only man has a soul.

It would be misleading to leave the impression that there is a sharp and unbridgeable cleavage between man and his biological predecessors in this or any other respect. The first predictive beginnings of what in man becomes a soul are identifiable in lesser breeds. We have noted some of them in the paragraph above. Had we been present on earth a billion or two years ago—just we, not humanity at large—we could scarcely have anticipated then where all these faint and fragile beginnings were destined to lead. Now, however, in retrospect the line of emergence is clear.

It is equally clear that patterns appear in evolution to all who examine the facts with more than just a microscope. Evolution seems to be headed in the direction (a) of order, (b) of cooperation, (c) of individualization, (d) of freedom and (e) of spirit. At least so far as this earth is concerned, man represents the highest measure of achievement thus far in each of these directions.

▼ *An Educated Guess*

What would happen if tomorrow every existing form of life were to be erased from our earth? It would be presumptuous in the extreme to pretend that any of us can at present know the answer. We can only guess. Or better: we can only extrapolate from the known to the unknown. My own guess is that—unless in the process of destruction the surface and atmosphere of the earth were to be rendered inimical to life—the evolutionary process would begin anew. I believe the same Creative Urge which was responsible for the evolutionary development of the past would assert itself in the future. This does not mean that in the next attempt life would of necessity be a carbon copy of what we know it to be. Perhaps no—perhaps yes—probably no. Because the environmental circumstances could not be assumed to be identical, it is logical to suppose that the specific forms of life might well develop differently.

If I were to be born again—of the same parents, with the same chromosomes and genes, but in a different part of the world—I would turn out to be quite different in many respects from what I now am. In all likelihood I would dress differently, speak another language, observe diverse mores, perhaps cherish divergent ideals. The same life-thrust would be modified by a different set of circumstances. My essential nature as a human being would remain the same. Some of the garments of custom and culture would be altered.

Similarly, if evolution were to repeat itself on earth, I believe the same inherent directions or urges would be manifest. The form of living being to appear at a comparable level next time might or might not bear resemblance to me. But I believe that, like me, it would be a way-station en route to expanding dimensions of order, cooperation, individualization, freedom and spirit.

Did my rabbinic ancestors instinctively suspect that perhaps this is not the first attempt of life to establish itself on our earth? They said that God experimented with several worlds before our own. Each time He found the preponderance of evil over good to be so ominous that He had to destroy His handiwork. After this world had been created, "God saw that it was good" and permitted it to endure. At least the initial stage of the experiment had succeeded.

The implication of this chapter—to be hastily posited now and elaborated later—is that man's ethical aspirations no less than the physical structure of his body inhere in and evolve from the very stuff of which he is made. Dr. Berrill, whom we have already quoted in other connections, writes: ". . . life in all its fantastic forms, actions and potentialities is as much a property of the basic stuff of the universe as the matter and energy of a starry furnace."*

Thomas Huxley probably thought that he was negating religion when he wrote: ". . . man, physical, intellectual, and moral, is as much a part of nature, as purely a product of the cosmic process, as the humblest weed."† What he was really denying was not religion as such, but any form of religion which presupposes a deity who controls and/or interrupts the cosmic process from without. It is precisely the fact that man—in *all* his potentialities, physical, intellectual *and moral* —is a natural part of the cosmic process, which leads the modern religionist to conclude that the very nature of the cosmos itself includes something of moral reality. Which means to say, that the universe includes within itself God.

Julian Huxley carries his grandfather's point a bit further and provides a bridge to our next major consideration when he writes: "The evolutionary point of view . . . establishes the reassuring fact that our human ethics have their roots deep in the non-human universe, that our moral principles are not just a whistling in the dark, not the *ipse dixit* of an isolated humanity, but are by the nature of things related to the rest of reality—and indeed that only when we take the trouble to understand that relationship will we be able to lay down ethical principles which are truly adequate."‡

* N. J. Berrill: *You and the Universe,* Dodd, Mead and Company, 1958, p. 27
† T. H. Huxley and Julian Huxley: *Touchstone for Ethics,* Harper & Brothers, 1947, p. 45
‡ *Ibid.,* p. 256

5

More About Man

In examining the expanding scope of the universe and the possibility of life on planets other than our own, Harlow Shapley protests what he calls "our automatic egocentrism" and asks: ". . . should we not openly question the rather vain and tedious dogma that man somehow is something very special, something superior?"* What his query amounts to is a modern, scientific paraphrase of that propounded centuries ago by the psalmist: "When I behold Thy heavens . . . the moon and the stars which Thou has established, what is man that Thou art mindful of him, and the son of man that Thou thinkest of him?"

The ancient poet showed broader insight than Dr. Shapley, however, in that he encompassed both sides of the paradox rather than just one. For he added: "Yet Thou hast made

* *Of Stars and Men*, Beacon Press, 1958, p. 9

him but little lower than the divine and hast crowned him with glory and honor." Even as a frail and fragile by-product of one planet surrounding one of the many suns in one of a multitude of galaxies, man still is "something very special, something superior." To the best of our certain knowledge, he is the highest consequence thus far of a process which probably had its elemental beginnings some four to five billion years ago. He is the sum total of the past and a presage of what is yet to be. By examining man more minutely we can perceive not only what evolution has already achieved but something of its promise for the future as well.

It is important, in so doing, to be clear about the nature of man's superiority. It is in no sense physical. A dinosaur, cast-off of evolution when man was in mere infancy, could crush a human being with utmost ease. A race horse can out-run us without half trying. The eye of the dragonfly can revolve to see in every direction with greater ease by far than the periscope of a submarine. From the top of the Empire State Building—a height of 1250 feet—you or I would have difficulty in distinguishing a man from a woman; a hawk from that height can with no difficulty see a dime. My dog hears many sounds which are impossibly beyond the range of my ears. The salamander can grow a new leg whenever one has been lost and the worm, when cut in two, can sprout a new head. (Are these not finer attunements to environment and better mechanisms of biological survival than anything man can claim?) If the purpose and direction of evolution were merely physical, in many respects it has retrogressed with the appearance of man. It is not in the physical but in the spiritual realm that man leads.

In addition to encompassing a new dimension of development, the spiritual, man differs in at least two additional respects from his animal predecessors. First, he is the only form of life which is consciously aware of how he became what he is. Secondly, and as a direct consequence of the first, he is the only form that can deliberately influence the future development of evolution for better or for worse. The trees outside my open window and the dog sleeping at my feet are no less the vehicles of evolutionary progress than am I. But they are unaware of their role and I am privileged to be conscious of mine. They are passive instruments of the evolutionary flow. Whatever contribution they have made to its current has been the result of automatic mutations within them, of which they are not aware and over which they can exert no influence or control.

My position is altogether different. While I am far from certain or complete knowledge, I know a great deal about the mutations that add up to myself. And—most important and exciting of all!—I can retard or accelerate the progress which is yet to be. I can do this to some extent even in the biological sense. The techniques of cross-breeding and selective breeding, of hybridization and eugenics, of medical science and hygiene, all enable me to become increasingly an active agent rather than a passive instrument of evolution. And the area of novelty, the sphere of the spiritual which points most promisingly toward the future, is exactly the realm where my potential influence is greatest!

All of which means that man is the first conscious partner of God in the process of evolution. If God is conceived as the Emergent Energy, the Creative Power, the Dynamic Force responsible for evolution—prior to the appearance of man He has been able to fulfill His purposes alone. From this point on, the consummation of the evolutionary goal depends upon God and man together. Neither can succeed any more alone. Man can help immeasurably in developing those traits of the spirit—of conscience, reason and creativity—which mark the next upward step of life. Or he can, by refusing his cooperation to God, bring the whole experiment to a woeful, catastrophic close. This is a frightening responsibility placed on the shoulders and heart of man. It is also a magnificent opportunity.

"It is as if man had been suddenly appointed managing director of the biggest business of all, the business of evolution—appointed without being asked if he wanted it, and without proper warning and preparation. What is more, he can't refuse the job. Whether he wants to or not, whether he is conscious of what he is doing or not, he *is* in point of fact determining the future direction of evolution on this earth. That is his inescapable destiny, and the sooner he realizes it and starts believing in it, the better for all concerned."*

The one emendation I would add to this elegant expression of the matter by Huxley is that man is not quite the sole "managing director" of evolution. It may safely be presumed that the Creative Power which operated in and through the process before man made his appearance is still actively present. Without that Power, man would be helpless to pursue a successful outcome. But without man's intelligent cooperation, the Power itself can no longer succeed alone either. In words recorded by the Talmud long centuries before any scientific notion of evolution had dawned in the human mind, "man is the partner of God in the work of Creation."

If man is a bridge between past and future, he is also a ligament between beast and God. Physically he is an animal, much like many other animals. Spiritually he comes closer than any other creature we know to resembling God. Jewish tradition seems to have grasped this with uncanny acuity. One of the ancient rabbis said that when God reached the sixth day of Creation He was in doubt about the kind of creature to have dominion over the earth. He feared to fashion just another beast because it would be aware only of

---

* Julian Huxley: *New Bottles for New Wine*, Harper & Brothers, 1957, pp. 13 f.

coarse physical experience. At the same time He was reluctant to hand dominion over to the angels because He was bored with their doing nothing but praising Him. His decision was to create a new kind of creature, man, who would be a combination of both.

Elsewhere another rabbi said: "In four respects man resembles the creatures above, and in four respects the creatures below. Like the animals, he eats and drinks, propagates his species, relieves himself and dies. Like the ministering angels, he stands erect, speaks, possesses intellect, and sees." This dual nature of man—the physical and the spiritual, and the inevitable conflict at times between them—may in no small measure be responsible for the alarming amount of emotional illness he has had to suffer.

▼ *Before We Leave Ourselves*

There is more yet to be said about man before we leave him. For one thing we must decry most vigorously the trend of our time to elevate God by depreciating man. This is, I suppose, a normal reaction to the tendency of the nineteenth century to glorify man excessively. While neither extreme is an accurate appraisal of reality, that of disparaging man's potential is clearly the more dangerous and unhealthy of the two. Skilled teachers and wise parents know that a child will often move toward becoming whatever self-image of expectation his elders give him. In this respect, none of us ever completely ceases to be a child.

Tell a man often and emphatically enough that he is a worm, and he will soon begin to act like one. Tell him he is trapped by Original Sin, foredoomed even before birth to be a miserable sinner, and he will be one. Remind him, frequently and explicitly enough, that he has the capacity to be but "little lower than the divine," and he will move toward that. My closest, most precious friend is a man who never fails to spur me on to greater accomplishment and fulfillment. This is because each time we are together he shows me an image of myself which is far better than I am but close to what I would like to become. I return from each visit with him convinced that if he thinks that highly of me, I must strive to fulfill at least some small part of his expectation.

Too many theologians today think of man and God as the two sides of a seesaw. In order for the God-side to be elevated, the man-side must be depressed. I hold this to be dangerous and enervating nonsense. For me the relationship between God and man is far more accurately and productively represented by the hands of a clock. They are identical neither in size nor speed. But the ratio between them is proportionate. It is impossible—without impairing the normal operation and usefulness of the clock—to increase or decrease the speed of one hand without correspondingly altering that of the other. So it is with man and God. Anything which lifts man glorifies God. Anything which debases man profanes God. This is true because man, so far as we know, is God's noblest accomplishment thus far, the sensitive spot in the universe where the finite physical comes closest to reflecting Infinite Spirit. Many years ago I heard Dr. Henry Slonimsky say: "Anything that lowers man's stature and diminishes his responsibility is an assault against God." I believe that to be true.

By any interpretation of Scripture—new or old, symbolic or literal—it is impossible to disparage man without belittling God. We are told that man is created in God's image. One cannot add to the lustre of the artisan by bemeaning His product, especially when that product is estimated to be the very crown of His creativity.

I am not the first to note a significant sequence in one of the early stories about Abraham. The eighteenth chapter of

Genesis begins: "And the Lord appeared unto him . . . as he sat in the tent door in the heat of the day." Immediately the text continues: "And he lifted his eyes and looked, and lo, three men stood opposite him." Abraham saw something of God in his fellowmen. We can too. The best in a human being is the closest we can come to an approximation of the Divine.

Because so many men have failed to understand that, too much of contemporary theology is an attempt at escape from reality and responsibility. The religious literature of our day is blighted by an abdication of reason and a panicked flight to mystic faith. The revolt against reason takes many forms. Whether in Christian existentialism or Jewish hasidism or Zen Buddhism—all popular vogues of our time— it adds up to the fact that since reason has manifestly failed to solve anything like our total problem, it is rejected out of hand. Perhaps the real trouble is not that reason, having been tried, has failed, but rather that it has never been adequately tried! The mind is at best a relative newcomer in the evolutionary procession. By itself, unaided by the heart, it can never provide total answers. But neither can answers valid for the modern mood be achieved without it.

I would hope not to be misunderstood here. The opposite extreme—that of abjuring faith in favor of reason alone— would be scarcely less disastrous. We need faith. Man cannot live by reason alone; but neither can he live without reason. His mind—part of his spirit or soul—has evolved at immense cost through millennia of evolutionary experiment in response to the Creative Energy which is God. It is one of his most precious instruments for perceiving God. It must not be contemned.

Reason without emotion and intuition may be compared to food which is entirely without seasoning. What is needed is a properly proportioned admixture of condiment. To substitute a plate full of pepper and salt for food is no answer. To reject reason in complete surrender to emotion or blind faith is to deprecate both man and God.

Of course we need faith to carry us beyond the bounds of reason. But that faith must be built on a foundation of reason, must be consistent with the reasonable and the known, not contradictory to them. If the direction of the knowledge yielded by experience and reason be represented by a solid line, faith must be a dotted line which continues in the same general direction, not one which goes off at a capricious and contradictory angle. My experience and knowledge show me that my wife is a superior person, a woman of deep loyalties and exquisite sensitivities. Therefore I believe—on faith— that she remains true to me even when thousands of miles separate us for a long and anxious year.

My study of evolution shows me specific and consistent directions in which life has developed up to this present moment. Therefore I believe—on faith—that unless man stupidly interrupts the sequence, as he now for the first time is able to do, the process will continue in similar directions. What I see and know of the universe convinces me that it is a process of order and meaning. Therefore I believe—on faith—that even those aspects of universal experience which I cannot fully comprehend must possess order and meaning. In all of these cases—that of my wife, of evolution and of the universe—the end result of faith is dependent upon and consistent with the foundation of reason.

All of which is perhaps a clumsy and complicated way of saying that I do not believe man possesses any avenue to truth which is superior to his reason. There are other avenues, of course: keen intuition, warm emotion, creative insight. But reason must never abdicate to any of these. All must be retained together—complementing and supplementing each other—if man is even to approach the wisdom of which he is capable.

Another word on the relationship between man and God:

Often it has been said that first man learns to love God; then, having learned that, and knowing that his fellowmen are created in the image of God, he is able to love them. Psychologically, I suspect, the direction is rather the reverse. First man needs to acquire a wholesome respect and acceptance of himself. Only then can he really love his fellows. And only then can he understand what it means to know and love God. Again the words of Jewish tradition are pertinent: "If a man says that he loves God but does not love his fellows, do not believe him."

▼ Are We Really Free?

At an earlier point in our discussion, when we spoke of freedom as one of the persistent directions of evolution, we deliberately begged the question of how free man really is. It sufficed at that stage simply to assume that, whatever we mean by freedom, man has more of it than does any other form of plant or animal life.

There are those among us who would voice reservations at this assumption. They would suggest that perhaps man's impression of freedom is really an illusion. An earlier generation of scientists used the lexicon of deterministic mechanism. They insisted—or some of them did—that man has no more real freedom than the rock or tree; that he too reaches his apparently "free" decisions only in response to certain forces from without and certain biochemical pressures from within —all of which are entirely beyond his power to control. More recently the restrictions on human freedom have been understood as psychological rather than biological. Each of our actions, we are told, is as inevitably and irrevocably the sum total of all prior actions as the solution to a problem in addition is the total of all the figures being added. And each decision we make is the only possible consequence of the conscious and unconscious pressures which emanate from our past. Far from being free, we are the doomed prisoners of heredity and environment.

I would not presume to insist that my answer to this grim inventory of man is the only one or that it can be proven either true or false in the laboratory. I believe it with my whole heart, but would not deny that it stands on the dotted line of faith which extends beyond the line of the known. I believe that man, a paradox in so many ways, is a paradox here too: that in some respects he is a prisoner and in other respects free.

Surely he is the prisoner of nature's laws, as all creatures are. It is impossible for him successfully to evade or defy these laws. Without some mechanical contrivance, he cannot breathe under water, no matter how hard he tries. Without a helicopter or plane, he cannot fly by the motion of his arms despite his most urgent effort. Yet this is only part of the truth. For it is man who decides whether to build a submarine or plane, and man who determines whether, once built, they should be used for good or for evil. In short, within the confines of nature's laws and constrained by these laws, man has freedom to make decisive choices. If it is true that in part his freedom is limited by biochemistry, it is equally true that he can understand and use that biochemistry. If unconscious conflicts from the past limit his freedom in the present, he can, by identifying and understanding these conflicts, emancipate himself at least partially from their imprisonment.

I may possess a certain amount of ability to express myself and be hopelessly incompetent in mechanics. My friend may be a genius at diagnosing a sick motor yet find it difficult to complete a coherent sentence. But he and I both are free to use or to waste our capacities—he to be or not to be a superior mechanic, I to write polished, finished sermons or to preach carelessly. Man is not wholly free. But neither is he wholly enslaved. He is the freest form of life that nature has yet been able to produce on our planet.

Once more the insight with which Jewish tradition perceived this truth long centuries ago is astounding. According to the Talmud, "the angel appointed over conception . . . takes a seminal drop, sets it before the Holy One . . . and asks, 'Sovereign of the Universe, what is to become of this drop? Will it develop into a person strong or weak, wise or foolish, rich or poor?' But no mention is made of its becoming wicked or righteous." Elsewhere the Talmud elaborates: "All is in the hands of Heaven except the fear of Heaven."

Maimonides was among the many post-Talmudic authorities who expressed themselves in the spirit of the Talmud on this point: "God does not decree that a man should be good or evil. It is only fools and ignoramuses . . . who maintain that God decrees at a man's birth whether he shall be righteous or wicked. Any man born is free to become as righteous as Moses, as wicked as Jeroboam, a student or an ignoramus, kind or cruel, generous or niggardly."

What Maimonides and the Talmud state as a matter of philosophic speculation or intuition, Dr. Sinnott expresses as a consequence of his scientific investigations: "Man does have motive power that is his own. He is not simply at the mercy of external agencies, strong and compelling as these obviously are. On the river of circumstance he still is borne along, but he moves there not inertly, like a log, but as a boat moves that contains within it power enough to give it steerage way at least, and sometimes even to carry it upstream against the current."*

This line of understanding leads inevitably to the rejection of fatalism. If every eventuality in my life, including the time and nature of my death, is predetermined in advance, then I am stripped bare of all freedom. Then I am reduced to a marionette, pulled and pushed this way and that by strings

* Edmund W. Sinnott: *Biology of the Spirit*, Viking Press, 1955, p. 77

of outer circumstance and inner compulsion entirely beyond my own poor power. In that event, evolution and life would be a grim, ghastly joke. If I have freedom—even within the severe strictures of natural law—then I have a vote in determining my own fate.

So we have seen what man is and how he became what he is. And we have at least glimpsed the Creative Power which relates him to all existence as its mortal crown. Our quest has brought us very close to the discernment of Wordsworth:

> And I have felt
> A presence that disturbs me with the joy
> Of elevated thoughts; a sense sublime
> Of something far more deeply interfused,
> Whose dwelling is the light of setting suns,
> And the round ocean and the living air,
> And the blue sky, and in the mind of man . . .

6

Time for Inventory

Now let us see where we are on the main highway of our argument and just how far the supportive discussions of the last chapters have carried us toward the understanding we seek. Our principal business has been to investigate the extent to which the underlying truths symbolized through the ages by belief in God remain tenable for our time. Let us, then, be reminded of what these truths were previously discovered to be.

1. Our universe is characterized by law and order, by purpose and plan.

2. Man is himself part of this plan. His life assumes its deepest significance from that affiliation.

3. Man is a spiritual as well as a physical being.

4. The universe which is man's host is also infused by spiritual or extraphysical reality.

5. Whatever man's part of the cosmic plan may be, it can be fulfilled only by deliberate action on his part.

6. There is something in the universe which helps man, which supports his own best efforts toward the meeting of this responsibility.

Perhaps it should have been noted when we traced these meanings initially that though they can be easily schematized for purposes of sequential discussion, in fact they are so closely interwoven one with the other as to be well-nigh inseparable. This should be apparent as we consider them further now. Our examination of evolution would surely indicate that the first three of them are at least as true today as when our forebears first conceived them. What primitive man somehow sensed on these matters by mystic intuition, his modern descendant has confirmed by exact scientific knowledge. Thus far, however, we have not yet inquired whether those universal forces which have revealed themselves in evolution are purely physical or partake also of the spiritual nature we have observed in man.

It is interesting in this connection to note how philosophy has swung through the centuries from one extreme to its opposite. For long periods of time many of the world's outstanding thinkers, following in the footsteps of Plato, were persuaded that the material world is an illusion, a pale reflection, as it were, of an ideal or spiritual world which constitutes the only reality. In the latter nineteenth and early twentieth centuries the tendency shifted toward believing instead that the universe (and everything in it, including life) is purely material, that all can be reduced to the kind of chemical reaction which takes place in a test-tube. Which comes closest to our understanding of the universe today?

Essential to the line of thought we shall pursue in attempting to answer this question is the fact that man is a part of the universe and human nature is an aspect of nature at large. We know that physically there is no element or combination of elements in man which is not found in the universe outside man. Which means to say that nature provided in advance all the physical raw materials essential for the ultimate appearance of man, who is her noblest product. If tomorrow the biochemist were to discover within man some new physical element hitherto unknown, it would be necessary from a scientific point of view to assume that this element will yet be found somewhere in the universe apart from man. One of the ancient rabbis showed how clearly he understood this when he said: "All that the Holy One, blessed be He, created in the world He created in man."

Not only is this much true, namely, that every physical element within us had to exist in the larger universe first, but many of man's capacities and functions can be understood only as reactions to established characteristics of the universe. For example: in order for sight to appear in pre-human and thus ultimately in human evolutionary forms, light-waves first had to exist as a pre-condition in the universe. It was in response to these light-waves that certain creatures began in the dim, remote past to develop small areas of skin that were especially sensitive to light. In the course of time it was these sensitive areas which developed into the eye which enables us now to see. Had light-waves not pre-existed, sight would never have developed. We can now confirm this sequence additionally from the fact that certain moles which live their entire lives underground and species of fish whose life-span is spent only in subterranean waters never developed functioning eyes, though they may possess the requisite physical apparatus for them, simply because they never came into contact with light. Again, therefore, one can reason backward and assume that wherever a living organism has developed a capacity to see, light was of necessity a part of that creature's environment first.

▼ Reflections of Reality

Very well, then, let us take this relationship between man and his universal environment a step further. We have already seen that there is a spiritual or extraphysical aspect to man also. Though this non-material side of him is inextricably tied in with and dependent upon the physical operation of his brain and glands and metabolic combustion, it goes obviously beyond the physical phenomena in which it is of necessity grounded. To think of it as being exactly synonymous with the physical would be as misleading as to say that electric current is identical with the wire which carries it. The current may be borne by the wire and dependent upon it but it also transcends it. So it is with man's body and soul. Even as the organic emerged out of the inorganic to become something quite different from and superior to it, even as the conscious emerged through and beyond the unconscious, and the self-conscious out of the conscious —so, with the appearance of man on this earth, does the strictly physical begin to emerge into the physical plus spiritual.

This is evident in many areas of human experience. In music, for example. Carlyle once defined a violin solo as the scraping of a horse's tail over a catgut. So far as it goes, this is an accurate description. Even the composition of music involves various kinds of physical activity: the electro-chemical operation of brain cells, the use of fingers on a keyboard or vibrations on one's vocal cords, the writing of notes with pencil on paper, and so on. But who would pretend for a moment that the creation and appreciation of music is only a physical experience? Clearly it involves the physical plus spiritual dimension to be found on this earth only in man.

Nowhere is this more convincingly apparent than in man's capacity to love. Physically, except for the fact that they generally face each other in the act, the sexual union of male and female human beings is no different from that of the male and female of any other species of mammal. There are even some few animals and birds which are monogamous—which develop an exclusive sexual relationship of significant duration between one male and one female. The moose lives with only one mate at a time, the hawk with one for a given breeding season. The wolf is faithful to his mate for life but will turn to a replacement if she dies. The wild goose will not select a second mate even if the first perishes.

But these instances are a far, far cry indeed from the full meaning of love in human life. Each physical union of husband and wife should deepen the spiritual attachment between them. Their love involves a sharing of everything which is truly important in human experience. The more this sharing extends beyond the physical to embrace also the intellectual, the cultural, the spiritual—the more beauty and meaning does a particular marriage encompass. To deny or repress the physical foundations of man's life is naïve in theory and unwholesome in practice. To deny the spiritual superstructure which emerges from these foundations, however, is to disparage man inexcusably.

Only one thing remains now to complete our line of reasoning. If it be true that physically man is a response to and a product of the universe which is his home, that every element within him exists somewhere in the vast scheme of things beyond him, why isn't it logical if indeed not imperative to believe that the same thing must be true spiritually? That there must be non-material elements also, akin in some respects to those we find in ourselves, which exist as part of the very fabric and nature of our universe—which are, so to speak, the raw materials of man's conscience and spirit and mind.

What we are saying here is that if a human being is more than a test-tube, the universe must be more than a laboratory.

If man possesses something that can be called spirit, there must exist a Universal Spirit of which his highest capacities are a product and reflection. Dr. Edmund Sinnott, whom we have quoted several times before, brings us the witness of a scientist on this point too: "The very existence of spiritual qualities in man suggests that they are manifestations in him of something like them in the universe outside. . . . Man's spirit, rooted in life, may actually be a part of the Universal Spirit, emerging from it and returning to it again."* Even Julian Huxley, who shies away from the word "spiritual," comes close to saying the same thing in his own way: "A further necessary postulate is that there are mental as well as material properties of the universe."†

It is interesting to observe here—is it not?—how once more modern man, acting on a premise quite opposite that of his ancestors, comes upon the same conclusion. It was once assumed that because God exists, which means to say, because there is a spiritual essence in the universe, therefore man too must have a soul. We today, schooled in science, are more apt to say: since a spiritual dimension of reality is discernible in man, therefore there must be its prototype or counterpart in the larger universe. Though opposite in direction and approach, the two premises lead to one conclusion. Both we and our universe are recognized to consist of considerably more than just the physical stuff of which we are manifestly made.

▼ *Ethics: Made by Man?*

It remains now to give attention to the fifth and sixth of our underlying meanings of God. These we shall consider in order inverse to their original listing: first, whether there is

* *Biology of the Spirit*, Viking Press, 1955, pp. 162, 164
† *Evolution in Action*, Harper & Brothers, 1953, p. 30

something in the universe which reinforces man's moral strivings; and then, the nature of his religious responsibility in the light of our modern understandings.

Before inquiring whether our ethical values are of firmer substance than man's own imaginings, let us deal for a moment with the values themselves. It is often said these days that all ethics are relative to the society in which they appear, that none therefore can rightly be labeled superior to others. The Eskimo believes it his duty to end the earthly life of his aged while we strive to prolong as much as we can the lives of ours. Each, we are told, is ethically proper for its own time and place. In certain Eastern lands it is considered part of a host's responsibility to offer a male guest one of his wives for the night; to us this is the height of sexual insensitivity. Neither, it is said, is ethically more admirable than the other. Both are acceptable and correct in their respective contexts. There is no objectivity in ethics.

The logic exhibited here is specious in the extreme. The fact that different civilizations diverge in their ethical standards no more removes the possibility of judging them inferior or superior than does their multiformity in other matters. There may well be certain backward areas where, even in the second half of this sophisticated century, the earth is believed to be flat. We do not blame those who are thus deluded but neither do we allow their ignorance to becloud our knowledge. We simply conclude that in scientific understanding some societies are clearly more advanced and learned than others. The same thing is true aesthetically. There are primitive civilizations whose achievement in other respects may equal or even surpass ours but whose musical standards haven't advanced much beyond the jungle drum. Do we say, then, that because of this deviation in taste it is wrong to judge the magnificent Chorale of Beethoven's Ninth Symphony superior to their chants?

There is, of course, an element of relativity in ethics, as

there is in science and aesthetics. But there are also objective criteria in all three areas. Later we shall turn our minds toward the nature of such criteria in modern life. For the moment, suffice it to say that they exist. The foolishness of pure relativity is illustrated by the story of the small community in which every day a mysterious call was made to ask the telephone operator for the correct time. After this had happened over a long period, the curious operator asked one day: "May I know who you are and why you call each day for the time?" "Sure," came the answer. "I'm the man who blows the town whistle every day at noon and I just want to be sure I'm doing it correctly." The operator burst into laughter and said: "That's wonderful, because we set our watches each day by the town whistle!"

The divergences in ethical values to be found among human groups today are due precisely to the fact that here too a kind of evolution has occurred. Some societies have evolved to a higher ethical level than others. They are no more to be praised than the others are to be blamed. Both should be accepted for what they are and all should be encouraged to develop even higher, guided by the best ethical insights the human mind and heart are able to devise.

Are these insights related to anything permanent in the nature of the universe? I believe they are. In an earlier chapter we observed that the evolutionary process itself—in moving toward order, cooperation, individualization, freedom and the spiritual—gives evidence of what might be called cosmic grounding for our ethical values. Now it is time to push this thought a point further in its development. Perhaps an analogy between physical and spiritual experience will help. From a physical point of view it is perfectly obvious that the circumstances and conditions of our universe are congenial to man's existence and development. We generally take for granted a multitude of such physical preconditions to man's survival. For example: our earth has to be located almost exactly its actual distance from the sun in order for life as we know it to develop here. A little closer, too much heat would have burned off the possibility of life; a little farther, lack of heat would have frozen it to extinction. The proportion of oxygen in our earth's atmosphere had to be almost precisely what it is now. Only a slight shift in either direction would have made life as we know it impossible.

The same thing is true concerning our ethical experience. There are ethical pre-conditions also, analogous to the distance of the earth from the sun or the proportion of oxygen in the atmosphere, which make it possible for man to create ethical ideals and to pursue them with a reasonable assurance of success. All of which means to say that man's moral values are more than the imaginings of his own mind, more than an independent exercise in futility, more than a dream destined for doom. Man's moral values correspond to an aspect of Ultimate Reality. There is something in the universe which makes it possible for man not only to envisage great ideals, but in substantial part at least to realize and achieve them. Our ethical propensities, no less than our physical bodies, have evolved as inherent characteristics of man's nature in response to something in the nature of the universe.

Matthew Arnold referred to this "something" as the "Power, not ourselves, that makes for righteousness." I would be happier had he called it the Power, greater than ourselves yet within us, which makes for righteousness. But the important thing, in his words or mine, is to recognize the existence of such a Power. Many men have perceived or at least sensed it.

Rabbi Ira Eisenstein has expressed it this way: "Belief in God means believing . . . that the ideals . . . we cherish are real, that justice, peace, brotherhood, compassion and honesty are not merely convenient arrangements which society somehow works out, but that these values actually emerge out of the very structure of the universe."*

* *Judaism Under Freedom*, Reconstructionist Press, 1956, p. 34

7

Moral Law: Fiction or Fact?

We begin to see, then, that for modern man too a long, deep look at the universe discloses something in it which seems to reinforce his ethical ambitions. We are not orphans of the universe ethically any more than we are physically. Not only does nature itself make ethical improvement possible, it encourages—nay, almost seems to demand such improvement. Another and perhaps clearer way of saying the same thing is that there is a moral law in the universe analogous to the physical law we all know. Take, for example, the law of gravity. No man can successfully defy the law of gravity. None of us can pretend it doesn't exist or bend it to suit his convenience. Even when we fly a plane or fire a satellite beyond the earth's gravitational pull, we are not thumbing our noses at the law of gravity—we are using what we know of its orderly and unvarying operation to accomplish the desired ends. We are remembering and demonstrating the words of Francis Bacon: "Nature to be commanded must be obeyed." I can jump off the Empire State Building in rude defiance of gravity only once. Nature will never give me a second chance.

Man does not create the physical laws of the universe. All he does is discover them and, if he be wise, conform to them as closely as possible in the living of his life. These laws existed before man ever became aware of them—indeed, it was precisely in response to them and consistent with them that man made his appearance. To the extent that we understand them and cooperate with them, we increase the probability of our survival and welfare, both individually and collectively. We ignore or forget them at our peril.

All this is easily understood in terms of *physical* natural law. It becomes more difficult to comprehend and more complicated to follow, but no less true to reality in terms of *moral* natural law. Here also there are patterns of reaction and behavior inherent in man, not dependent on him for their creation but available for him to discover, with which he must conform in order to live a happy or successful life. The fact that here we are inquiring into human behavior rather than that of the universe at large should not mislead us. Human nature is no less important a part of nature than are the planets and stars. Law discernible in man's relationship to himself and his fellows is no less an aspect of natural law than is law operating in the winds and tides.

Nor should we be foolishly deceived by the fact that the results of disobedience to this kind of law are not always as immediate or dramatic as they would be if I were to jump off the Empire State Building. Even contempt of physical natural law may be either immediate or deferred. If I defy it by swallowing a large quantity of poison, it will be immediate. If instead I absorb smaller quantities of ac-cumulative poison over a long period of time, it will be deferred but no less lethal. If I plunge my unprotected arm into a pot of boiling water, the disastrous consequence is suffered at once. If I expose the same arm to daily doses of X-ray radiation, the consequence may eventually be even more catastrophic though I may for a time seem to be escaping it. The penalty for violation of moral natural law is more likely to be deferred and less likely to be apparent at once than that for defiance of physical natural law. But only a fool would for that reason ignore it.

The possibility that at least the larger directions of our ethical strivings are grounded in and consistent with the very nature of the universe is intriguing. It provides the very best premise we have for a modern ethic. It is, moreover, being increasingly recognized even by scholars whose basic orientation is not theological. Thus Julian Huxley writes: "The happenings of the cosmos contain the potentiality of being understood in the form of moral law, in relation to the concepts and feelings of rightness and wrongness."*

Lawrence K. Frank is even more explicit: "In his endless search for the democratic way of life, man can now find support from the universe, because the stars in their courses, the electrons and atoms proclaim that as the only way the universe continues to exist."†

▼ *Down to Cases*

Let us try to be even more concrete in comparing the two kinds of natural law. Suppose we think in terms of a newborn baby. The physical laws by which the parents of an infant must abide are known to everyone. They must provide their child, among other things, with sufficient nourishment,

* T. H. Huxley and Julian Huxley: *Touchstone for Ethics*, Harper & Brothers, 1947, p. 228
† L. K. Frank: *Nature and Human Nature*, Rutgers University Press, 1951, p. 44

with the proper variety of vitamins, with adequate oppor-tunity for rest. Any failure to comply with these physical requirements or laws will result in a child of stunted develop-ment and growth.

What, then, are the spiritual or moral laws governing the earliest years of a child's life? Primarily they revolve around and emanate from the need for love. A human infant is born with an almost insatiable hunger for love. I think it would be no exaggeration to say that the need for love is the primary spiritual law of human survival. If an infant be denied the love it needs—though it be supplied with every physical requirement in generous abundance—the result will be a stunting of emotional growth which can lead to crippling pain far into the future. It is no more possible to evade the inexorable functioning of this spiritual law without courting disaster than to ignore the law of gravity.

Let us carry the analogy a point further now into adult life. All of us are aware of the physical or biological laws we must observe for the sake of healthful survival. If we disobey them—by exposing ourselves to infection, by drink-ing to excess, by living in filth, by inadequate diet or rest—we know we are asking for trouble. What we are only now beginning to understand is that the same risk is involved when we choose to defy the moral laws which are also, so to speak, built into human nature. Again the law of love comes to mind. Perhaps we have concentrated too much on the need *to be loved* and too little on the need *to love*, too much on the effect of hate in its victim and too little on what it does to the hater.

More than once I have watched hate consume the hater with inexorable viciousness. A friend of mine committed suicide without ever lifting a finger of physical violence against herself. She did it by hating her father with such bitterness and envying her friends with such spite that she poisoned herself as truly as if she had swallowed a bottle of arsenic. No physical medicine succeeded in helping her. Perhaps psychiatry could have at an earlier period of her life, but only by freeing her to comply with the law of love instead of defying it.

Man's need to be essentially honest is another example. In his essay, "The Luxury of Integrity," Stuart Chase tells of an accountant who was approached by a government tax official who offered surreptitiously to hand him the names of corporations which had not yet been informed that the government owed them rebates. The accountant was to offer his services to such corporations on a commission basis. When notice of the rebate arrived, it would appear as if this were his accomplishment; he would then share with the revenue agent the fee received for his "work." He was tempted by this lucrative possibility until his mother, with whom he shared his dilemma, reminded him of her difficulty in awakening him each morning and said: "I'd hate to come into your room and find every morning that you're awake already."

Dr. Paul Johnson has captured the truth implicit in this incident. He writes: "The need for open honesty is in the long run quite irresistible. As Jung has said, nature will punish the man who does not come clean and openly declare his honest feelings and intentions. The burden of concealment and deception is too grievous to bear, and eventually men break under it one way or another. To live a lie is so contrary to human nature that our personal integrity cannot tolerate it, and we either confess or disintegrate in neurotic evasion and despair."*

An example of what guilt can do was reported by one of our international news agencies just about the time these paragraphs were being prepared. In July of 1954, a thirteen-year-old boy was killed by a car in Illinois. A man who had

* Paul E. Johnson: *Psychology of Pastoral Care*, Abingdon Press, 1953, p. 107

been driving while drunk near the scene and at the time of the accident had no recollection of having hit anyone but there was a dent on his front bumper which he was unable to explain. For five years, according to the press report, he kept "the haunting fear locked within his conscience. The worry became so intense that he became irritable and his wife, Violet, left him two years ago taking their two children." Finally, the inner torment became so unbearable that he turned himself in to the police.

The role of guilt in human behavior is one which requires much additional study by both religion and psychiatry. This is not the place nor am I the properly qualified person to undertake such study. It should be observed and remembered, however, that, contrary to popular impression, it is not the purpose of psychotherapy to erase all guilt from the human heart, even if that were possible. There is healthy guilt and diseased guilt, wholesome guilt and devastating guilt. There are circumstances and times when we should feel guilty. Our guilt is often nature's way of punishing us for disregard of her moral laws.

Guilt which is unconscious or imaginary or out of all proportion to an actual misdemeanor should, of course, be ventilated and reduced to size. But guilt which is realistically related to an actual offense is man's way of knowing that he has, wittingly or otherwise, defied the moral law.

I know the rejoinder of many at this point. It will be objected that the punishment which emanates from this kind of tension is made by man, not by nature. And if man would refrain from producing guilt in his children and himself, this sort of punishment could be avoided. But if man were to do that, he would no longer be man! To suggest otherwise is to forget that man alone has developed the conscience and ethical values which sometimes lead to guilt and that he has developed these as an expression of his unique human nature which is—let it be repeated—an essential aspect of nature at large. We can no more disregard this kind of natural law than any other.

We are barely at the threshold of recognizing the relationship between ethics and mental health. Erich Fromm is among those who have challenged us to a deeper understanding of this relationship. He writes: "My experience as a practicing psychoanalyst has confirmed my conviction that problems of ethics cannot be omitted from the study of personality, either theoretically or therapeutically. The value judgments we make determine our actions, and upon their validity rests our mental health and happiness. . . . Neurosis itself is, in the last analysis, a symptom of moral failure. . . . In many instances a neurotic symptom is the specific expression of moral conflict, and the success of the therapeutic effort depends on the understanding and solution of the person's moral problem."*

▼ *Let's Be Practical*

We who emphasize the importance of ethical behavior are often accused of being impractical idealists, of living in an unreal dream world. If we urge the application of ethical principles to the pursuit of profit, we are told that "ethics are ethics and business is business." If we plead for the cessation of nuclear testing, it is immediately objected that we live in a practical world of enemies where such idealism isn't feasible. A clear understanding of moral law will enable us to understand that actually the "idealists" are the only truly practical people. In the long run ethical conduct is the only kind which succeeds.

Sex is as good an area of human experience as any in which to illustrate how true this is. We have already referred to the fact that sexual intercourse, which in animals is a purely

* *Man For Himself*, Holt, Rinehart and Winston, Inc., 1947, p. viii

physical experience, can become in human life a physical pleasure with rich spiritual overtones. For long centuries it has been asserted in our kind of civilization that because this is true both pre-marital and extra-marital sexual intercourse should be avoided. It would be foolish to deny that often this advice is honored in the breach. I have heard physicians speak of the human sex need as if it were purely a physiological urge. In one case a young widow in my congregation came to me deeply disturbed because her doctor had advised her to satisfy her sexual hunger with no more qualms than if she were filling an empty stomach or scratching an itch. He would have been among the first, I am sure, to agree that in some circumstances one doesn't indiscriminately proceed even to satisfy his hunger for food or to relieve an itch.

To treat sex this way is to cheapen human life, to accept from man in this extremely important area of life a standard of behavior which belongs on a lower rung of evolution. It is impossible to treat sex exclusively as a physical phenomenon for the years between adolescence and marriage and then suddenly, because of a few motions and words of ritual, to transform it into an experience which is both physical and spiritual. Nor can the husband who has indulged in a purely physical extra-marital sexual adventure this week go through the same experience with his wife next week on a very elevated spiritual level. All this has been urged in one way or another for centuries. And all this has been accepted for centuries in theory and often rejected in fact as "impractical."

Now for the first time, as our studies of marriage become more scientifically reliable, we begin to see that, not merely in theory but in fact, man's chance for happiness increases as he acts in accordance with the very real differences between his own nature and that of animals. Contrary to the "practical" advice, circulated and accepted with such certainty, that sexually experienced men make the best husbands,

careful studies indicate a positive correlation between chastity before marriage and happiness in marriage. Thus Terman, one of the pioneers in studying the factors associated with successful marriage, concludes: "One's chances of marital happiness are at present favored by the selection of a mate who has not had intercourse with any other person."[*]
Dr. Paul Popenoe, President of the American Institute of Family Relations, has written: "As is well known, all studies show that the happiest marriages are between persons neither of whom has had any previous sexual experience."[†]

Clarence Leuba, for many years Professor of Psychology at Antioch College, tells us: "Investigations of happiness in marriage indicate that those who were virgins at the time of marriage or who had had intercourse only with the person whom they eventually married were happier on the average than those who did not fall in either of these two categories."[‡]

The quotations and conclusions can be multiplied. The late Dr. Abraham Stone, founder and for many years Medical Director of the Planned Parenthood Federation of America, approached marriage not on idealistic but on intensely practical, scientific grounds. His conclusion? "I should personally speak out strongly against any form of sexual promiscuity. Considerable clinical experience and contact with young people has impressed me with the fact that indiscriminate sexual relations endanger the wholesomeness and balance of one's personal and social life. In spite of our changing values, it seems to me that a lasting union of one man with one woman is still the most ideal form of human sex relationship."[¶]

[*] L. M. Terman: *Psychological Factors in Marital Happiness*, McGraw-Hill, 1938, pp. 327-9
[†] *Modern Marriage*, The Macmillan Company, 1940, p. 175
[‡] *Ethics in Sex Conduct*, Association Press, 1948, p. 82
[¶] Lawton and Archer: *Sexual Conduct of the Teen-Ager*, Spectrolux Corporation, 1951, p. 170 f.

This counsel is confirmed by many others, among them a psychiatrist and a religious writer who recently collaborated in a cooperative study of their respective fields. They write: "Sexual intercourse is but one item in a total human relationship, and it provides emotional fulfillment only as it is an expression of mature love between a man and a woman in marriage. Advice that overlooks this is likely to have dangerous results."*

The reason why this is true, while immensely pertinent and important, need not detain us here. The point to be emphasized in our present context is that marriage and sex provide a vivid example of moral law as it actually operates in human life. When men are true to the highest and best in their nature, their chance for happiness is proportionately increased. When they settle for too much less than their best, in this or any other area of behavior, the long-run prognosis for their welfare is not good.

The perceptive reader may be able to think at once of dramatic exceptions. Forgetting for a moment that many of these exceptions may be more apparent than real, more temporary than permanent, let it not be denied that such instances do in fact exist. Shall we recommend them, then, as good examples in the quest for happiness? There have also been cases reported of men or women who never used a toothbrush or visited a dentist, yet whose teeth are in perfect condition. The person who wants to enhance his chance for happiness would obviously be ill-advised to take such exceptions as his guide. The general rule is that dental hygiene leads to oral health. The general rule is that ethical behavior leads to long-range happiness. The general rule in both instances derives from the wisdom of complying with natural law, in the one case physical, in the other ethical.

This is true not because God looks upon each action of

* Linn and Schwarz: *Psychiatry and Religious Experience*, Random House, 1958, p. 143

every human being and decides when and in what manner punishment should be dispatched, but because nature is so constituted that, in the words once more of Edmund Sinnott, "by the inexorable laws of life, some conduct carries its own reward and some its own penalty."* Elsewhere Dr. Sinnott has been more explicit: "The penalty for wrong biological behavior is pain. Failure to attain those moral and spiritual goals which the experience of the race has found to be the highest brings more subtle forms of pain and grief."†

He who ignores a sign warning him not to touch high tension electric wires will be electrocuted. Not because the supervisor in the powerhouse becomes angered and directly punishes him, but because he has ignored the nature of reality. The punishment is inherent in the deed. He who foolishly attempts to live in disregard of nature's moral laws will be punished in the same manner and for the same reason.

Early tracings of the idea that punishment and reward are natural rather than supernatural phenomena are found in Judaism. Even the Bible speaks of nature bestowing her bountiful blessings on those who live ethically, while denying them to the sinful. In the Bible, to be sure, the natural and supernatural are almost hopelessly intertwined. We today would certainly not accept the premise implicit in such Bible verses as the following from Leviticus: "*If* ye walk in My statutes and keep My commandments, and do them; *then* I will give you rains in their season . . ." We do not believe that the conduct—ethical or unethical—of any individual can alter or affect the weather. Yet we have seen how nature —on the whole and in the long run, even if not in each minute operation—will serve those who obey her more beneficently than those who attempt to defy her.

In seventeenth-century London, a Spanish rabbi was accused of equating God with nature. A colleague ruled in his

* *Matter, Mind and Man*, Harper & Brothers, 1957, p. 173
† *Biology of the Spirit*, Viking Press, 1955, p. 122

favor on the ground that God's punishments and rewards come to us *al derech ha-teva*, by means of nature!

In short, the patterns of nature are such that water exposed to temperatures below 32 degrees Fahrenheit—if at sea level and at rest—invariably freezes into ice; and normal human flesh exposed to temperatures above a given degree inevitably feels pain. The patterns of human nature are such that conduct which is consistently and flagrantly unethical causes distress, while that which is ethical increases the probability of happiness. This is what modern man means when he affirms the existence in his universe of something which works for him in his struggle toward moral goodness.

The pedagogical implications of all this are immensely important. Perhaps one reason our ethical instruction has had less impact than it should is that we have too often offered it in the guise of authoritarian pronouncements rather than as crystallizations of actual experience. The Ten Commandments as arbitrary rules issued by God or Moses—by parent or teacher—will have less effect on the conduct of the next generation than if they be presented as rules which by and large carry their own consequences to the welfare of the individual. In short, the best of our ethical insights are results rather than premises—results of millennial experience through which man has learned enough about his own nature to know that only by conforming to it can he earn a reasonable prospect of happiness.

This does not mean that an ethical person never suffers. We intend to deal with this later in discussing the entire problem of suffering and evil. For the moment, suffice it simply to enter on the record this *caveat* against a naïveté which should not be permitted to fester through the intervening chapters.

8

How Do We Find the Right Way?

Only one of the persistent meanings men have expressed through their otherwise changing ideas of God remains now to be evaluated in terms of our contemporary knowledge of the universe and ourselves: the conviction that we must undertake certain specific modes of action on our own initiative if our portion of the universal plan is to be fulfilled.

This was the weakest link in the chain of nineteenth-century liberalism, which abused the notion of moral law by supposing that ethical progress is automatic and inevitable. It assumed that the universe is like a stream, the current of which flows firmly in the direction of ethical improvement, and that all we need do is relax in our canoes while the current carries us to the swift triumph of our most precious ideals.

Both the concept and the analogy were mistaken. It would have been more accurate to think in terms of a surface of water which upholds us, which sustains us and enables us to make progress toward the goals we seek if—and here lies the essential crux of the matter—*if we undertake the effort* necessary to exploit the conditions favorable to our moral advancement. There is no automatic guarantee of moral improvement. There is rather a Power in the universe which makes such improvement possible, which promises that our ethical dreams are not doomed to disappointment.

A simile may be helpful here. Electricity is a quality or property of the universe in which we live. It was a part of nature's armamentarium no doubt from the beginning— in all events, long before man first discovered it. The fact that some men in the remote jungles of earth are as yet unaware of electricity in no way diminishes either its reality or its potency; it exists despite their ignorance. Once men had discovered the presence of electricity as a property of the universe, they then faced three alternatives. They could ignore it. They could use it to their frightful harm. Or they could harness its power to their blessed advantage. Electricity will do nothing for man until, first, he himself has discovered its existence, and until, secondly, he has exerted his ingenuity and energy to harness it.

In much the same way, though with the necessary inadequacies and imperfections of every analogy, those of us who believe in God are convinced there is a Force in this universe which might be called, so to speak, spiritual and moral electricity. It exists even among and within those men who are oblivious to it. It enables us to dream our noble visions of ethical perfection and to reach out toward these visions with the possibility of success. It means that when men are at their ethical best they are attuned to something close to the heart of Reality itself.

The worst perversion of religion is to minimize even for

a moment man's responsibility to cooperate with this Force. In his struggle—not always successful—to avoid such perversion, man has, since the dawn of moral consciousness, sought to distinguish between evil and good. Usually he has done this in terms of pleasing the gods or God. We would be wise now to define moral goodness as realizing our own highest potential and contributing our best to the on-going process of evolution. Whatever man does to boost life upward in its restless urge toward advancement is ethically good. Whatever action he takes to the contrary is evil. Each of his choices or decisions must be measured against this yardstick.

If it be true that evolution has tended in the directions projected earlier and that man possesses the conscious capacity to accelerate or retard these tendencies, then his responsibility becomes clear. The most important—and rewarding—thing he can do is cooperate with the Creative Power active within the evolutionary process to the end that the pace of this process be speeded. We would do well, then, to recall the directions of evolution and to ask ourselves in what way we have the power to expedite their accomplishment.

The first of these directions was from chaos to order. To perceive fully the implications of this for human conduct it must be remembered that in nature the individual particle moves toward order only as it becomes associated with other particles in a larger aggregate: the proton, the neutron and electron in an atom; the atom in a molecule; the molecule in a piece of lumber or steel or flesh. There would be no order of any consequence in a finger or leg that had been amputated from its body. Nature's order is achieved only through integration of the individual into the whole.

This is also man's first clue to moral responsibility. His individual life takes on added meaning and order precisely as it becomes related to other lives, each a cell in a larger social body. The larger the whole of which I am a part, the greater the order in my life. If my efforts and desires are coordinated with those of my wife and children, there is more order than if I stand alone. As they become in turn channeled into those of my community, my city, my country and all humanity, the order is proportionately enlarged. One man striving by himself to discover the cause of cancer or win a battle or construct a skyscraper faces insuperable odds. His efforts, however intense, will fail to produce the order he seeks. But when men are counted together in thousands, though the tasks remain formidable or even foreboding, order (which means to say, success) becomes possible.

It follows that whatever a human being does to relate himself to other human beings in a cause common to all of them and consistent with additional criteria yet to be spelled out is a step forward in terms of ethical conduct. The qualification of consistency with other criteria is important. Otherwise it might appear that a group of a hundred men who conspired to commit murder were behaving ethically. Subject, then, to this limitation, that act is ethical which moves toward order through interrelatedness with others.

Our second criterion is closely related to the first, actually an outgrowth of the first. It will be remembered that order was achieved in nature only through cooperation and specialization. Enough has been said above to indicate that this is equally true of human behavior. To the extent that —like the protozoan—I live wholly for myself, or—like the parasite—I take constantly from others but offer nothing in return, I am unethical. The wider the scope of my symbiotic relationships, the more I contribute in some ways to the welfare of others while at the same time depending upon them in other ways for my own well-being, the more ethical my conduct becomes.

We have already observed that the "egotistic" cell produces cancer. It remains now to add that the man or woman who pursues only his own narrowest and most immediate interests, who refuses to find his greatest value and gratification in his contribution to the welfare of the larger group, is a social cancer, no less fraught with disastrous consequences for society than is a biological cancer in the human body. Cooperation must be added to order as an index of morality.

Pierre Teilhard de Chardin carries his biological observations quoted earlier to their logical and spiritual conclusion: "No evolutionary future awaits man except in association with all other men. The dreamers of yesterday glimpsed that. And in a sense we see the same thing. But what we are better able to perceive, because we stand on their shoulders, are its cosmic roots, its particular physical substance, and finally the specific nature of this mankind of which they could only have a presentiment—and for us not to see this we have to shut our eyes."*

The third direction discernible in evolution is the apparent paradox that as the single cell subsumes itself in favor of the larger organism it increases its own uniqueness and importance. We called this individualization. Its implications for ethical conduct are obvious. Within the very minimum of restriction necessitated by survival of the group and of humanity at large, non-conformity is a value cherished by nature.

When Dr. Albert F. Blakeslee retired as President of the American Association for the Advancement of Science, he said: "Individuality is the kernel of democracy, the biological basis of the struggle for freedom. When we fight for individuality we fight on the side of nature."†

Whoever seeks to impose conformity on others is there-

* *The Phenomenon of Man*, Harper & Brothers, 1952, p. 246
† New York *Times*, December 30, 1941

fore acting contrary to one of nature's predilections. Any act calculated to force all men to dress alike, speak alike, vote alike, think alike or believe alike is thus an unethical act. The politician who brands every deviation from his own views subversive is unethical no matter how impassioned or pretentious the patriotism in the name of which he presumably speaks. The clergyman who insists that the only road to salvation is to believe precisely what he believes—that any divergence is heresy—is unethical despite the divine sanction he invokes. This is true, not simply because the Declaration of Independence or the Constitution of the United States proclaims it, but because it follows ineluctably from the innate, intrinsic direction of evolution.

▼ *Additional Signposts*

The fourth direction of evolution was found to be freedom. Every act which increases the prospect of freedom, for myself and my fellowman, is an ethical act. Every act which unnecessarily constrains my freedom or his is unethical. The greater the freedom I can help bring into the greatest possible number of lives, the more ethical I have been. Within the individual this means freedom from the tyranny of unconscious resentment or guilt. In the family it means freedom from domination of children by parents or parents by children or husband and wife by each other. In society it means freedom from all the cruel enslavements which men foist upon their fellows in the name of race or color, of class or creed.

Freedom for the many at times requires some restriction on what appears to be freedom for the few. It may be necessary to deny the wealthy or the bigoted "freedom" to live exactly as they prefer, in order to increase the possibility of freedom for others. The speed demon must be denied the "freedom" to drive as fast as he wishes or no one will have freedom on the highway. The man who is certain that he has found the one exclusive key to truth must be prevented from forcing the key on everyone. Such restrictions can be justified on more than just the mathematical balance between the few and the many. For in the end freedom which hinges on exploitation of the helpless and weak ceases to be freedom even for the powerful and strong.

The kind of freedom which is most important as a criterion of ethical action will become clearer as we turn to the fifth and most significant direction of evolution, the development from the physical to the spiritual. This is man's greatest margin of superiority over all other earthly forms of life. The more he strives to expand this margin, for himself and for others, the higher his level of ethical achievement. This does not mean abnegation of the body or its delights. For man to deny the physical enjoyments he shares with the animal kingdom is as faithless a betrayal of his true nature as to deny the divine, which means to say, the spiritual potential within him. Both forms of denial are false and falsity is immoral. Judaism teaches that in the end each man is accountable for the legitimate pleasures of life of which he failed to avail himself! Being true to our superiority as human beings means not denial of the physical, but such enjoyment of it as will add also an element of spiritual appreciation and growth.

One can enjoy eating or sex relations as a purely physical experience. To do so is willfully to remain arrested on the animal level and thus to be unethical. Or one can, while enjoying the physical satisfaction of his hunger for food or for sex, transform it also into the spiritual joy of creating stronger family loyalties, deeper devotion and love. What a crude distortion of the human potential it is to suppose that all sexual intercourse which follows a wedding ceremony is moral. Husbands and wives who use each other's bodies solely for sadistic aggrandizement are sexually immoral no matter how many prior words of pious ritual have been pronounced over them.

Each of my actions is moral to the extent that it pushes the frontiers of my experience outward from the purely physical to encompass the spiritual as well. This is another way of asserting that whatever I do to reinforce the progressive development already manifest in evolution is ethical. Whatever I do to inhibit that development is unethical. Whenever I take a positive action to discover or understand truth, to create or appreciate beauty, to follow the dictates of my conscience, I am, so to speak, pushing evolution another notch upward and thereby fulfilling my moral responsibility.

Spinoza had something very pertinent to say on this point. He proposed that virtue consists of being what one essentially and uniquely is. Virtue in a horse, if there were such a thing, would therefore consist of being the best and most highly developed kind of horse possible—in emphasizing and refining those special characteristics which make a horse different from any other animal. Spinoza said specifically: "A horse would be as much destroyed if it were changed into a man as if it were changed into an insect."

It follows, then, that virtue in man consists of developing to their utmost potential those qualities and characteristics which are unique to human beings. Man is virtuous, according to Spinoza, only to the extent that he stresses his uniqueness by deliberately pursuing truth, beauty and goodness. Whenever he makes a decision, however apparently insignificant, which moves him in the direction of these goals, he thereby and to that extent not only achieves virtue, but also plays his part in the further development of evolution, which means to say, in the fulfillment of life's ultimate purpose. He becomes a conscious partner of that Power which is at the heart of all existence and life.

Properly understood, this means that virtuous conduct will not of necessity be the same for all of us. The shoemaker who, possessing the potential for making the best shoes in town, turns out work that is indifferent and shabby, is unethical. The painter with genuine artistic ability who squanders his talents shamelessly is also unethical. But no ethical opprobrium can in fairness be directed against the shoemaker who fails to paint or the artist who refuses to make shoes. Each of us is responsible for the development and fulfillment of his own human potential as an individual.

▼ No Easy Way

This kind of approach to an understanding of good and evil is not an easy one. It would be far simpler and more convenient to have a chart on which each individual action could be identified in moral terms. Just as we follow a vertical column down and a horizontal line across a travel chart and at the point of confluence discover the exact distance between two cities, how pleasant and comfortable it would be to guide all our conduct by such certainties. Or to turn in each instance to an authority, as our progenitors did for so long, and be guided by his domination. But this is not the way of maturity and growth. It is certainly not the way of expanding freedom. It is the path which emerges from yesterday, not the one which leads to tomorrow.

If man is to fulfill his ethical promise, there can be no substitute for careful, at times even painful thought. We can offer him a compass with which to find his way, not deep ruts which will carry him automatically to his destination. Each moral dilemma he confronts must be resolved not in terms of dogma but according to guide-lines suggested by nature itself. Which course of action before me is most productive of order and expressive of cooperation? Which enlarges the boundaries of individualization? Which will confer a deeper dimension of freedom on the largest number of individuals involved? Which will strengthen most our unique spiritual capacities as human beings? All these taken together amount to asking: how can I consciously, deliberately align my conduct in conformity with those ethical directives for which nature itself has already indicated an affinity? No one will deny that our specific ethical objectives as we ordinarily articulate them are products of mankind's creative mind. But we fail to approach anything like the whole truth unless we recognize that in working toward these ends our minds are attuned to and expressive of something very real in the universe itself.

Even when the right questions are asked, the answers will not always be easy. Often the choice is not between good and evil but between varying degrees of both. How do we act, for example, when truth and love conflict? Do we speak truth to the terminal cancer patient, thus compounding her anxieties and fears? Or do we tell a deliberate lie in order to act with love at the cost of betraying truth? It is only within a larger context which encompasses more than these two ideals as such that a solution can be found. That course of action is correct which, according to our wisest judgment and in the long run, seems best calculated to promote rather than to impede the advance of evolution.

▼ *Is the Golden Rule Enough?*

Here we come upon a question which is being asked with increasing frequency. If religion is to be judged so largely in terms of its ethical consequences, why do we need it today at all? After a building has been completed the temporary scaffold used in its construction is discarded. At a certain stage of man's adventure, it is said, religion served as a useful device for the encouragement of morality. Men who might otherwise have acted sinfully could be impelled to behave properly because they were convinced God wanted them to and would punish them if they did not. But have we not outgrown that time, it is asked; and should we not now be able to do good without the prospect of cosmic punishment or reward? Why do we require a substructure of theology? Why can't our religion just be the Golden Rule?

It would be both dishonest and unfair to deny that agnostics or even atheists can be and have been highly ethical persons. But there is great difference between living ethically just as a matter of good sportsmanship or social utilitarianism and living ethically because one is convinced that thereby he helps consummate a universal plan. It is the difference between hammering nails into boards because one thereby helps the merchants of wood and steel to earn a living and hammering them because one is thereby building a house.

The right ethical choice often entails harsh sacrifice. It may necessitate the surrender of much material gain or the opprobrium of one's friends or risking death in the performance of duty. How willing one will be to pay the price of such decisions may well depend on how much one believes to be at stake. If I am acting just on the mundane level of the greatest good to the greatest number—worthy as that limited objective may be—my threshold of sacrifice is likely to be far lower than if I believe my decision will help determine the outcome of a cosmic adventure. And my ability to absorb disappointment and tragedy will also be less.

Rowing a boat by myself for the exercise it affords is a commendable thing to do. Rowing with others in a crew to bring honor to my school is even more admirable. Rowing to rescue a swimmer in distress is more creditable yet. Rowing a refugee from tyranny across a river to liberation because I am convinced that freedom is one of the purposes of my being alive is the most meritorious of all. In each case exactly the same muscles and motions are involved. How meaningful they are depends upon the width of their context. Religion extends the widest possible context to my ethical choices, thereby giving me the greatest incentive to act decently. It offers me values and ideals which are not merely my own creations but which inhere in nature and evolution.

Samuel Rosenkranz has expressed with great sensitivity the contribution of religion to the ethical person: "If there is no meaning in the universe to ignite the meaning in the individual life, then there is no support for human effort and no assurance that upon his death . . . all the work of his heart and hand will not be utterly destroyed. . . ." If, on the other hand, there is universal meaning, "then meaning in a human life becomes not the expression of a lonely soul fighting a lost battle in a dark and hostile world, but the song of a courageous worker expressing purpose in a universe friendly to his ideals."*

It should not be surprising by now to discover that here too our modern insights were adumbrated long ago by Jewish tradition. One of our ancient rabbis said: "He who performs a moral act, as for instance, a judge who pronounces a righteous judgment, associates himself with God in the creation of the world."

In another tractate of the Talmud we are told that in the beginning God's Presence, the *Shechinah*, resided on earth. When Cain sinned, the *Shechinah* withdrew to the lowest level of heaven. When Enoch sinned, it ascended another notch. Thus each generation's misdeeds drove God, as it were, farther away from earth. But for each sinner, the Talmud continues, there was a corresponding righteous man. Thus Abraham by his good deeds brought the

* *The Meaning in Your Life,* Philosophical Library, 1958, p. 59

Shechinah back from the seventh to the sixth level of heaven. Isaac restored it to the fifth and Jacob to the fourth and so on until Moses brought God back to earth itself. When men fail to act like men rather than ingenious beasts, they divorce themselves from the deepest, most precious meanings of the universe. When they strive for the holiest and the highest, they reunite themselves with God.

▼ *Pardon Our Sins*

In our lexicon of modern religious meaning what do forgiveness and atonement mean? In an older vocabulary they signified that if a sinner truly regretted his transgression, if he voiced his dismay and sincerely vowed not to err thus again, God would forgive him as a parent forgives his wayward child and would give him another chance. Usually there were also certain prescribed rituals to be performed. From time to time strange examples of these still come to light. On August 9, 1959, the New York *Times* reported that "an ascetic Indian is accomplishing an unusual penance in Ceylon to gain peace and grace. . . . He is somersaulting and does not intend to stop until he has covered at least fifty miles. He has already covered thirty-five miles and natives drop in prayer as he passes by." Many of the rites still practiced by allegedly modern men for the purpose of penance are scarcely more congenial to our state of knowledge than the Indian's, though admittedly more sophisticated.

Sometimes—as in Judaism—forgiveness was contingent even more on man's meeting his obligations than on God's grace. We are told, for example, by the rabbis of old that God will not forgive an injustice perpetrated against one of our fellowmen until restitution has been made for the damage inflicted and the injured party has forgiven first.

And that atonement is not complete until the sinner is exposed to the same temptation again and resists it! This is a long step forward in the direction of mature atonement, one which deserves to be carried even further.

It will help us do this if we turn our minds back for a moment to our earlier discussion on the two kinds of natural law, the physical and the moral. Would it not fit reality to suggest that defying the physical law of nature is an error, while defying her moral law is a sin? If, while hunting, I carelessly trip and fire a bullet through my foot, I have defied a physical law of nature. I have committed an error. No one—unless he believes that hunting itself is immoral— would accuse me of sin. If, on the other hand, I fire the same gun at my companion because he has angered me, it is clear that I have defied both the physical and the moral laws of nature. My misdeed is so much more severe than in the first instance that this time it is no longer merely an error; it assumes the dimension of a sin.

We do not customarily use theological terms like "atonement" when a physical law of nature is defied. Yet it may help us no little to realize that much the same sort of procedure is in order in both incidents described above. What would an intelligent approach be in the first case, that in which I was a victim of my own carelessness? The first step would be to assess the amount of damage done and take steps to repair it. This might range all the way from a quick dash of iodine to a tourniquet and extensive stitching, or even amputation, dependent upon the amount of injury inflicted.

A second step, in order only after completion of the first, would be an inquiry into the causes of my unfortunate accident. What had I done wrong? Was my gun cocked when it should not have been or my attention distracted from the business at hand or my knapsack so loosely slung that it forced me to fall? Why did I unintentionally violate a physical law of nature?

The third step would be the most important of all. Having arrested or repaired the damage and evaluated the cause of my mistake, I would then try to learn from this experience enough to prevent its recurrence. Which means to say: I would try not to defy the same physical law of nature in the same way again. If, when next I found myself in similar circumstances on a subsequent hunting expedition, I avoided such an accident, my "atonement" would be complete.

It would do me no good if, in lieu of these three steps, I simply sat on the ground bemoaning my fate or piteously beseeching God to help me. God could not have saved me from the consequences of my folly unless I took certain measures myself, unless I used my own intelligence and exercised the capacity to learn from mistakes with which He has endowed me. Alexander Magoun has expressed something closely akin to this thought with his characteristic perspicacity and humor: "An automobile will not run because of the threat to leave it outside the garage on a winter night. Nor will it run because of the promise of an extra quart of high-grade oil at Christmas time. It responds only to treatment which is honestly based on a respect for its true nature."* So, to "atone" for the accident which injured my foot, I must try to understand my own true nature and that of my gun and that of the universe in which I live and the interaction among all of them. And I must try to conform in my future conduct to what I discover to be true.

Now what of the second case, that in which sin is involved because I have defied not only the physical law of nature but her moral law also? Why should my procedure be any different in this instance from the first? Again, my

* *Cooperation and Conflict in Industry*, Harper & Brothers, 1960, p. 86

immediate concern must be assessment of the damage I have caused and its speedy repair. Next comes the question of what caused me to do what I did. Here the answer will not be so simple as a cocked gun or a loose strap or momentary distraction. I may have to dig down deeply and at length into my own self—my tensions, my resentments, my conflicts, my guilt—before I can begin to identify the real target at which I was firing when I shot my friend. Only on the basis of such understanding as this can I ever forgive myself; only as a consequence of forgiveness by myself can I assume that God has also forgiven. The third step would in this case follow almost automatically from successful completion of the second. Once I had discovered the reason for my violent aberration, I should then be able to prevent its recurrence.

What part does God play in this process? God is the Energy which has so created and infused the universe and myself that I have intelligence and will enough to discover the causes of my errors and sins, to correct them and to avoid repeating them. God is the Force which keeps the universe operating in such stable sequence that I can anticipate the results of any given course of action; under identical circumstances it will be the same tomorrow as it was yesterday or today. God is the Moral Power which so orders human nature and experience that in the long-run I can be happy only to the extent that I conform to the highest within me. God is the Healing Spirit which enables the tree to survive a broken limb or the salamander to grow a new leg or me to forgive myself and survive my guilt, provided I understand it and deal with it productively. If there were no God—called by this or any other name— each mistake would be a tragedy and all life would be a grim joke. Because God is and I am able at least in part to perceive Him and depend upon Him in my moments of contrition and shame, atonement is possible. I can be "at one" with my own true nature and that of my fellowmen and that of the universe which has spawned us. Mistakes can be corrected. Guilt can be obviated. Man can learn and grow and mature and become more like God.

9

The Crux of the Matter at Last

Where are we, then, in our excursion toward a mature faith for tomorrow? We have dug down as deeply as we could beneath the surface of men's perennial ideas about God to discover the essence of what they believed and were attempting to say. And upon examining at length each of the essential meanings of belief in God, we have discovered it to be no less cogent and appropriate for our time than it was in the past. Yet something is still glaringly wrong.

It would be foolish to pretend that when most people today use the word *God* they have explicitly in mind the truths we have been specifying in the last few chapters. The trouble is that we have been using a vocabulary and a conceptual framework which are threadbare to express ideas which are eternal. We rather successfully avoid doing that in all areas of human experience except religion. We no longer think or speak about thunder and lightning as people did ten or five or even two thousand years ago. Thunder and lightning operate today exactly as they did then. But where they were once believed to be manifestations of divine anger, today we understand their natural causes and speak and act accordingly. If we still based our research and conduct in connection with thunder and lightning on our remote forefathers' concepts, we would be dealing with something very real and consequential in the universe but in a manner altogether divorced from today's knowledge, hence irrelevant to reality.

We would, moreover, be subjecting ourselves to needless danger and harm. It was once believed that the most effective way of protecting a community from lightning was to ring the church bells in the midst of a storm. Such conduct did nothing to protect the community though, to be sure, it increased the risk for the one person delegated to climb the church tower, there to tug at the bell cord. We must not be too harsh toward those who behaved so foolishly at a time when man's knowledge of his universe was still severely limited. But what would we say of those who, with today's knowledge available to them, still hoped to combat storms with bells?

We need not go back so many centuries for examples. Our own grandparents utilized the principle of the wheel for purposes of transportation. So do we. But they used carriages and we use automobiles. At first, indeed, they called their motor vehicles "horseless carriages." We have long since dropped this quaint and one-time descriptive label. And we would immediately commit to a mental hospital any man who hitched a horse to his new Chrysler and carried a whip as he struggled into the driver's seat. In short, we still recognize and utilize the same basic principle for land transportation as did our ancestors but we achieve far more effective results because we do not restrict ourselves to their knowledge or language.

Men once believed that by certain kinds of human conduct they could avert the danger of floods. We still believe this today. But where past generations attempted to accomplish this end by performing a variety of rituals and ceremonies, we do so by conserving forests and building dams. For us to utilize their language and methods would be to prostitute our exalted position in evolution. Yet this is exactly what most of us do in our religious life. Because we have developed a fixation on modes of expression and conceptualization appropriate to earlier and less knowledgeable centuries, we lose sight of the important essence which they expressed in their proper manner and which we must now learn to express in our own way.

There are two unfortunate results of our failure to follow in religion the wisdom we apply so generally elsewhere. One is that some of the brightest and keenest minds among us, failing to perceive the relevance of contemporary religious expression to reality, have discarded religion altogether. The other and no less lamentable result is that even those who retain a formal affiliation with religion find their professions of faith more and more divorced from life itself. It is this, I believe, more than anything else which accounts for the deplorable paradox with which we began our inquiry, the strange anomaly of increasing signs of religious "success" and decreasing evidence that religion really matters very much to most of us. The only cure I can see for these maladies is a bold, even if to some people disturbing, effort to chart out the changes we must explore in our ancestors' concepts of God if we are to express in a new idiom the same fundamental truths for which they were groping.

Many dangers lie ahead as we do so. It is possible to become ridiculous in the attempt to rephrase theology in contemporary terms. In January of 1958 a nationally known radio sportscaster preached the Sunday sermon in a Brooklyn church. The following morning one newspaper reported the event as follows: "Mr. Barber described the relationship between God and man as similar to that between a good baseball manager and his players. 'A manager gets his work done through his players,' he said, 'and God gets His work done through us.' "* We shall try to be less fatuous as we turn to some of the newer religious insights we need.

▼ *Person or Process?*

With varying degrees of literalness most men through the ages have conceived God as a Cosmic Person. To some extent I suppose this is inevitable, since we naturally tend to see all experience in terms of our own humanness. We do this when we speak of Mother Earth or call nature "she" or describe a tree as "reaching" toward the sky. I remember my professor of theology once saying that if fish were capable of religious speculation, they would probably picture God with fins and scales. So we have pictured Him (even the personal pronoun is a case in point) as a Person or, at the very least, possessing some of the traits of human personality.

There was a special temptation, almost a need, for men in earlier times to do so. After all, they were far less capable of abstract thought than we, less accustomed to thinking in terms of processes than of persons. The only kind of order and purpose with which they were immediately acquainted was human order and purpose. Therefore when they sensed these traits in the world of nature, they attributed them to the same sort of personality they knew in themselves.

In some measure each of us recapitulates the development of the race mentally even as we do physically. We know

* New York *Times*, January 27, 1958

that the human embryo goes through successive stages where it resembles fish and later apes on its road toward birth. After birth our mental progress also reiterates that of mankind. In early childhood we are individually no more capable of abstract thought than were adult men and women 200,000 years ago. Some of us can still remember that when we first heard human voices sounding from phonographs or radios we assumed there must be a person inside the box before us. Not yet able to comprehend the process as such, we used persons to symbolize electricity or electronics. Little children even go so far as to personify such inanimate objects as chairs or dolls, talking to them as if they were persons.

In much the same manner and for something of the same reasons, earlier man found it necessary to personify the forces he felt about him in the universe. He could understand a storm only as a cosmic temper tantrum, differing merely in degree from his own occasionally wrathful behavior. We have progressed far beyond that point as far as storms are concerned but still think too literally in terms of a Cosmic Person at a time when we should be capable of more abstract thought. The purposeful order we perceive in nature . . . the exciting though sometimes excruciating development from protozoan to man . . . the principle of organization which permeates and unifies every manifestation of existence from the remotest galaxy to the minutest cell within our bodies: all this we should now be able to conceive as Energy or Power or Force or Intelligence rather than Person.

This does not mean that we must immediately drop all personal pronouns, henceforth referring to God only as *It*. Any more than we are prohibited from ever again calling nature "she" or referring to the "shoulder" of a mountain. What it does mean is that we must be clear within our own minds, knowing when we speak literally and when with poetic symbol.

Does this mean that we no longer believe in a personal God? That depends on which of two possible meanings we ascribe to the word "personal." If it implies a God who is a Person, the answer, as far as I am concerned, is negative. I do not believe that God is a Person. I understand why it was once necessary for men to think so, just as I understand why men formerly clothed themselves in the skins of animals; but I find the past useful or attractive to me in neither respect.

If, on the other hand, by "personal" we mean a God who functions in our lives *personally*, my answer is decisively affirmative. The concept of God enunciated in these pages means much, much more to me in personal terms than any idea could of God as a Person. It performs for me precisely the purposes assigned to religion in an earlier chapter. It helps me understand the meaning of my life in universal terms, it moves me toward more ethical behavior by energizing a greater portion of my potential, and, in ways which remain yet to be elucidated, it assists me to survive the bumps and blows of life.

Rabbi Eugene Kohn has put the matter very well: ". . . to say that God is personal does not necessarily mean that God is a person. Many things that are not persons are personal—love, honor, friendship, loyalty. None of these ideals is impersonal; they have meaning only as they are manifest in personality. In that same sense, God is personal. God is indeed the very source and sponsor of human personality."*

This brings us to the brink of an exceedingly difficult kind of question. Does God, though not a Person, possess personality? There are those whose sense of logic dictates that He must. They would say that if God is the source of everything that has developed or will yet develop through evolution, the source cannot be less than its effects. Since human personality, which includes everything we have al-

* *Religion and Humanity*, Reconstructionist Press, 1953, p. 42

ready attributed to man's spiritual nature or soul, is the highest product of the source to this point, something closely akin to human personality, it is urged, must also be characteristic of the source.

Others who believe no less in God find it unnecessary to follow this line of reasoning. They would say that God can be the Force which reveals itself as human personality without even remotely resembling such personality. Electricity produces pictures in my television tube but electricity itself does not in the least resemble those pictures. The process of growth in nature produces roses from one kind of seed and cucumbers from another and men from another. In order for the process of growth thus to succeed, however, it need resemble neither a rose nor a cucumber nor me.

I find it quite possible to leave this matter unresolved without in any way disturbing my faith. To me the question of whether God does or does not possess personality (or as some would put it: whether He *is* or *is not* personality) is one which we shall never be able to answer and which is not the essential question in any event. The important thing is to recognize that God exists and to perceive how His existence can affect the way I live my life. Once that has been achieved, let men differ as widely as they wish on the problem of personality.

A question corollary to this is whether God is consciously aware of each individual in his actions. Does He know, for example, that I am sitting in the sun now writing these words and that tomorrow I shall dictate them for my secretary to transcribe? The answer each of us gives to this question will depend on the kind of person he is and on his own needs. Some, no doubt will find the notion of a God who is not conscious of the individual hopelessly remote and cold. I do not. I am indebted once more to Alexander Magoun for the thought that I do not expect the President of the United States or even the Governor of my Commonwealth to be aware of my location or conduct at any given moment. I do expect them to be generally aware of my needs as a human being and to provide for those needs as nearly as they can.

Similarly I am grateful beyond words to God for having created and sustained the kind of universe in which I could emerge as a man and, having emerged, can think clearly, feel deeply and act nobly. This is more than enough for me. If I am not important enough for the Governor of Massachusetts to keep track of my comings and goings, why should I require or expect such personalized attention from the Governing Power of the Universe? God can be with me and within me every instant of my life without keeping a pair of cosmic binoculars trained on me.

As long as eight centuries ago, Maimonides recognized the impossibility of describing God. We can never say what God is, he insisted. We can at best say only what He is not. The first prerequisite for a theology which will be viable in coming centuries is to understand that God is not a Person.

▼ Supernatural or Natural?

The second is to realize that He is not supernatural. At least not in the literal sense of being beyond nature, acting upon it from the outside. Rabbi Mordecai Kaplan, one of our generation's most creative Jewish theologians, has suggested "transnatural" as a more accurate adjective for God than "supernatural." Whether we accept his specific word or not, the important thing here is to think of God as operating within and through nature, permeating it from beginning to end, rather than activating it from without. The difference is crucial. Fire, baking a loaf of bread, is an external force applied from outside. Yeast, mixed with the dough itself, is an inner force, causing the loaf to rise. I mean no irreverent heresy in suggesting that God is the yeast of the universe.

It is not necessary to become a pantheist, to say that God equals nature and nature equals God, in order to hold this view. The lake which ripples a few yards from me and the breeze which causes its surface to move are parts of nature. But they are not God—only manifestations of God. The man-made satellite, whether it orbits or falls to earth, is not the law of gravity; it merely reacts to the law of gravity, showing us how that law, which we cannot see, operates. Thus nature is not God. It is suffused with God, responsive to God, energized by God.

When a rowboat is towed by a powerboat, both move in the same direction and at identical rates of speed. The first is activated by force applied externally. The second moves in response to power applied from within. But even in the second case, the motor is not identical with the boat. So nature is not identical with God. The old view conceived nature as entirely physical, infused with spirit by a source outside itself. What is suggested in our newer estimate is that nature consists of both matter and spirit together, indivisibly so. Science tells us that matter and energy are differing forms of the same essence, that matter is energy at rest while energy is matter in motion. It is time now for religion to recognize that matter and spirit, while they may not be quite the same, are nonetheless inseparable aspects of Ultimate Reality.

God is to nature what energy is to matter. He is within nature. He is not supernatural. I like the way N. J. Berrill expresses himself on this point: "We need no faith in supernatural forces. We need only to recognize that our knowledge of the universe through our senses and our knowledge of the universe through our own inward nature shows that it is orderly, moral and beautiful, that it is akin to intelligence, that love and hope belong in it as fully as light itself, and that the power and will of the human mind is but a symptom of reality; that we, when we are most human, most rational, most aware of love and beauty, reflect and represent the spirit of the universe."*

▼ *Magic or Order?*

At least one more ingredient is indispensable as we grope toward a concept of God for tomorrow. It is consistent with and follows logically from the two we have already considered. If God is not a Person, if His abode is within nature, not outside it—it must follow that twentieth-century religion leaves no room for magic. Expressed in these words, this assertion will doubtless gain unanimous assent. Yet if we say the same thing differently—that there are some things God Himself cannot do—many who have just agreed will voice vigorous objection. Why?

Because we have been taught since childhood that God's power is unlimited. The very suspicion that He may not be omnipotent after all is disturbing. Joshua Loth Liebman expressed the discomfort of many people in this connection and pointed toward a solution: "At first it seems daring, if not heretical, for us to say that God is . . . limited. We ask in amazement, 'How can God be limited? If He is not all-powerful—able to do anything that He wills—then surely He cannot be God!' I deny this conclusion. If I did not believe that God is *limited* by the very nature of the world He created, then I would have to surrender my faith."†

In discussing with the boys and girls of my Confirmation Classes whether God can interrupt or suspend His own laws

* *Man's Emerging Mind*, p. 286. Copyright, © 1955, by N. J. Berrill. Reprinted by permission of Dodd, Mead and Company
† *Peace of Mind*, Simon and Schuster, 1946, pp. 160 f.

of nature, I often ask: Which way makes God seem more wonderful? Which alternative would strengthen your belief in God? Though at first it seems to many of them that a God who could perform miracles would be more powerful than one who cannot, my hope is to help them understand that the opposite is true. If God could change the past or abrogate the law of gravity or cause it to rain in the absence of clouds, I could no longer believe in God because the principle of organization and causality and integration which men have perceived in nature would no longer be there. I believe in a God of order, not one of caprice or whim. I subscribe to Albert Einstein's statement that "God does not play dice."

Is it really a reduction of God's power to say that there are some things He cannot do? That God possesses all the power there is in the universe but some kinds of power may be nonexistent even for Him? It requires all of God's power to operate an orderly universe. Exceptions to the order of nature would bespeak less power, not more. The burning bulb in my lamp is evidence of power sufficient for illumination. If the lamp flickers and is extinguished though its filament is still operative, this is evidence of power diminished, not power increased. So, if there were exceptions to the orderly patterns of nature, they would bemean God's power, not exalt it.

In short, I do not believe in miracles. Not if the word be interpreted in its usual sense as exceptions to the laws of nature. I believe in miracles only as occurrences and events which are far too marvelous for me fully to comprehend but which are entirely consistent with nature's accustomed patterns. I believe that for God to have created the universe at its inception, to have sustained and evolved it through all the millennia since, is a miracle of incomparably greater proportion than had He in fact divided the Red Sea or sent manna from heaven in the wilderness.

Here we come upon another of those extremely sensitive spots where it may seem to some that I am on the brink of heresy. Yet there have been more than a few authentic spokesmen of Judaism in the past who have expressed their discomforts and doubts about miracles. One of the most telling rejections of miracles in Jewish tradition comes from hasidic literature. "Rabbi Bunam told this story: 'Rabbi Eleazar of Amsterdam was at sea on a journey to the Holy Land, when, on the eve of New Year's Day, a storm almost sank the ship. Before dawn Rabbi Eleazar told all his people to go on deck and blow the ram's horn at the first ray of light. When they had done this, the storm died down. But do not think,' Rabbi Bunam added, 'that Rabbi Eleazar intended to save the ship. On the contrary, he was quite certain it would go down, but before dying with his people he wanted to fulfill a holy commandment, that of blowing the ram's horn. Had he been out to save the ship through a miracle, he would not have succeeded.'"*

It is also possible, however, to conceive of miracles not as interruptions in the laws of nature, but as developments and phenomena ineffably beyond man's present capacity to comprehend. In this kind of miracle I do believe. For me a universe of constant law and order is a more magnificent miracle by far than would be one of occasionally spectacular disorder. There is a miracle of spectacular beauty in the design of every snowflake and in the fact that no two of them have ever been identical. There is a miracle in the fact that although a worker bee lives only about six weeks and a queen bee at most three years, a man or animal which befriended a bee colony can go back to it ten years later on a day when anyone else would be attacked and will be

* Martin Buber: *Tales of the Hasidim; The Later Masters*, pp. 247 f. Copyright, 1948, by Schocken Books, Inc. Reprinted by permission of Schocken Books, Inc.

received in safety by the descendants of bees long since dead.

The instinctual behavior of a newly hatched chick is also a miracle. It will ignore a duck flying overhead but react with stark terror to a hawk. How does it know the difference? The outlines of the two in flight are nearly identical. Their outspread wings are alike and the long neck of the duck corresponds to the long tail of the hawk. The only basis of differentiation is whether the long end precedes the short one or follows. So acute is the perceptivity of chicks in the first hours of their life that if a black cardboard silhouette of a gliding bird is pulled over a wire above them with the long end first, they ignore it: it's a duck. If the short extension comes first, they are terrified: it's a hawk!

Indeed, even before being hatched a chick gives evidence of miracle. Dr. Llewellyn Thomas Evans has told of standing by a batch of eggs on the fateful twentieth day when the unborn chicks had already commenced to peck their way out of the shell. A hawk appeared overhead. Suddenly the rooster swooped over the eggs, covering them with his wings and issuing a strange sound. At once the chicks stopped their pecking, remaining perfectly silent until after the rooster, by departing, had indicated that the danger was gone!

What else is it but a miracle that the entire present population of this earth, three billion of us, developed from egg cells that would fit into a one-gallon container and spermatozoa equal in volume to less than an aspirin tablet? Do you know any word more descriptive than miracle for the fact that within the tiny, sub-microscopic cell each of us was at the moment of conception were already contained the seeds of all the physical traits, all the mental characteristics, all the emotional proclivities, all the creative possibilities of the adults we are today? Compared to that, a sea splitting in two or a whale swallowing and then regurgitating a man is simple child's play. There are more miracles without magic in this universe than the wisest of us could ever identify. The trouble is that most of the time we're looking for them in the wrong places.

There is one more kind of miracle in which I believe— the miracle of the human spirit—what my late beloved friend, Rabbi Milton Steinberg, called "the achievement by spirit of what by every law of logic and common sense seems impossible." And he added: ". . . when the immovable is moved, when the insuperable is conquered, when the impossible is achieved, what else is that but a miracle?"

Is it necessary to illustrate in detail? In 1958 the wife of my most precious friend died in New York, eight years after her first operation for cancer, three years after it became apparent that the end was impending. Ten days before her death she was making toy animals for the children in the hospital and practically forcing her roommate to eat and trying to get the Negro who cleaned the room each morning to laugh. Elsie Rudin was a miracle.

I remember on the morning of February 19, 1945—D-Day at Iwo Jima—standing with a young Jewish boy at the rail of our ship just before his turn to go over the side in the first wave of attack. He was so horribly frightened he couldn't keep his entire body from trembling violently. Later I learned that upon landing he helped save another man's life and earned a medal for bravery. That boy was a miracle.

Such miracles as these neither depend upon magic nor require the suspension of nature's laws. They are the only kind in which I can believe. They disclose for me a God immeasurably more wonderful and awesome than one who could capriciously control the universe as if it were His toy.

To sum up, here is the three-fold context within which my concept of God must fit if it is to square with the knowledge of reality given me by science and if it is to function creatively in my life. My God is not a Person. He is not supernatural. He is not a Cosmic Magician.

▼ A Healthier Concept

Not only does such a concept of God square more accurately with reality, it also is more conducive to mental and emotional health. It has become popular in our time to emphasize the compatibility between religion and psychiatry. Too often we overlook the fact that while truly mature religion is indeed consonant with psychiatry, as it is with every discipline of science, there are some interpretations of religion which are destructive of health.

I remember an arresting example from my earlier years as a camp counselor. For several seasons we had with us a young boy who, for all practical purposes, had been reared more by an ignorant, superstitious maid than by his parents. She had filled his impressionable mind with all kinds of damaging nonsense about God, telling him that God was watching him every minute of the day and night, that God knew every evil deed, even every wicked thought of which he had been guilty, that God would punish him for every last one of his infractions. So effective had her instruction been that the poor boy would awaken at night screaming in terror that God was about to punish him!

Freud may have had experiences such as this in mind when he called religion a neurosis, a wholesale projection onto the universe of unwholesome dependencies we felt as infants toward our parents. In terms of the more traditional concepts of God there was considerable merit in Freud's view. Faith in an omnipotent, authoritarian, vengeful God can indeed infect the believer with unhealthy fear and guilt. If God is a capricious Magician who can do with me as He pleases, even to the point of abrogating His own laws, there is nothing I can depend upon in this universe for security. Such a God makes it all but impossible for me to develop my own inner resources and strength.

But God conceived as a creative, pervasive Spirit—within me as He is within all existence—establishing and sustaining me as He establishes and sustains all life—punishing me, when He does, not in capricious anger but in consonance with laws He has given me the intelligence to understand—rewarding me, when He does, as a consequence of the same laws—God thus conceived and understood reduces my guilt to reasonable proportions and improves my prognosis for happiness and health.

▼ Do We Need New Words?

It has been suggested that, because the concept of God developed in these pages differs considerably from that held by most people, to use the same word is to confuse rather than clarify. Perhaps, then, the word *God* should be retained for those who still think of Him as a supernatural, magical Person, and a new term be devised for those who assent to the kind of interpretation offered here.

Notwithstanding the semantic confusion which admittedly exists, I believe it would be a grave error to surrender the word *God* to the exclusive use of those who think more in terms of yesterday than of tomorrow. For one thing, to do so would be to overlook the fact that the meaning of the word has been subject to change from the beginning. This we observed at the outset of our inquiry. Perhaps there would have been an immediate, temporary advantage if a new term had been adopted when men first started to think of God as one and spiritual rather than many and physical. Or when they first reached the point of affirming that God is everywhere rather than restricted to a local residence.

These changes, in their way and at their time, probably introduced almost as much confusion as the changes proposed now. But if new words had been invented for each major change of concept, the eventual result would have been more confusion, not less.

The word *God*—whatever its transmutations and changes—has always referred to that which man believed to be Ultimate Reality. Whatever a given generation deemed to be responsible for manifest existence in the universe was always called *God*. Even if a satisfactory substitute were now to be devised, it would become necessary each time we used it to add in a footnote that what we really meant is what people ordinarily mean by *God*. It is better to keep the same word, thus maintaining a proper continuity in our religious development and expressing the very real progress we have achieved. In no event can all semantic confusion be avoided.

There are certain other words and phrases which have been associated with belief in God for so long a time that it is better to reinterpret them now than altogether to abandon them. For example: we speak of *God's will* or we say that *God wants me to* do this or that. What can such terms mean in our newer context?

When I say *God's will*, I mean the nature of the universe and myself. When I say *God wants me to*, I refer to my inescapable responsibility to conform to the nature of the universe and myself. Thus, *God wants me to* eat a balanced diet and breathe adequate quantities of fresh air and obtain sufficient rest and keep my balance while riding a bicycle. It is *God's will* that I love and allow myself to be loved, that I try to be as honest as possible with others as well as myself, that I endeavor to develop my noblest potentials in the pursuit of beauty, of goodness and of truth. I satisfy God's will in the exact proportion that I conform to the physical and spiritual laws of His universe.

How about *God watches over me,* or *the Lord is my shepherd?* These phrases express my modern religious mood insofar as they refer not to a Cosmic Parent but to the laws of nature which are changeless and dependable. To the extent that I discover and obey them, I shall be happy and well. In the measure of my ignorance or disobedience, I must expect suffering and sickness. When the physical and spiritual laws of life seem to have backfired, it is not that they have suddenly ceased operating. It simply means that I don't know as much as I should about them or that I haven't succeeded in my effort to observe them.

Thus, much of the vocabulary of prayerbook and psalm can be retained, provided that the words be reinterpreted in the light of modern knowledge and understanding.

We have raised more questions than we have answered. In the light of this newer interpretation of God, how can we explain human suffering, especially when it sometimes comes excessively to those who seem to strive most mightily for ethical improvement? What role is there, if any, for prayer? What, if anything, survives our death? No religion will endure which fails to offer its adherents reasonable replies to such questions as these. What answers are consistent with the premises already proposed?

10

The Valley of Shadows

"Why did God do this to me? . . ."

This is beyond doubt the most frequent question asked of me through the years by anguished congregants. I have come to expect it almost as a matter of routine upon entering a house of mourning.

Early one day some years ago a famous lung surgeon at the New England Deaconess Hospital phoned frantically for my help with the hysterical daughter of a patient who had just died. Upon reaching the hospital I encountered a young South American matron, oblivious to all in her immediate surroundings, refusing to leave her father's body, rocking back and forth almost catatonically as she moaned over and over again: "Why did this happen to me? All my life I have tried to live a good Jewish life. I say my prayers daily. I keep a kosher home. I never forget to light Sabbath candles. Why did this happen to me?" . . .

I stood one day at the graveside of a man who had died in his mid-fifties and whom I was helping to bury. His widow didn't hear a single syllable of the prayer I read. Neither did most of the other mourners. My voice was vanquished by hers, shrieking hysterically, almost defiantly: "O God, why did You do this to me? God, why didn't You listen to me?" . . .

The case studies could be multiplied almost endlessly. All in essence asked the same question: if religion has any meaning, if God is a good God and if I have faithfully attempted to fulfill what I believe His will to be, why wasn't I spared this aching pain? The question is altogether valid even if the premises out of which it issues are largely false. We agreed many pages back that the principal functions of religion, in addition to providing us with a meaningful interpretation of the universe and of life, are to spur us on to higher levels of ethical behavior, to encourage us toward releasing more of our latent spiritual energies and to help us over the inevitable bumps of life. For modern men the last of these, no less than the first three, must be cast in a religious context which shuns the supernatural and eschews magic.

No one who has stood, as I have more than once, at the grave of a tender little child, or sat through dreadful days and anxious nights with men and women strained to the breaking point, or buried the pitiful remains of fine young friends in combat, can deal with sorrow glibly or pretend for an instant that skillfully spun logic can altogether assuage the anguish of the human heart. Yet we must try. When the heart breaks, no less than when it sings, we cannot afford to abdicate our God-given reason. To whatever extent there are answers, in whatever measure comfort is possible, it must be in a world of reality, not one of fanciful escape.

We begin, then, by trying to clear out the accumulated

underbrush of superstition. Unless we commence with correct assumptions, there can be no hope of achieving valid answers. First to be dispelled is the axiom that human life, with or without religious faith, can be or indeed even should be lived without pain. To believe this is as irresponsible and unreal as to suppose that life could endure on earth if the sun were never darkened by clouds. Pain is in part and at times the lot of every human being. So it has always been. So it always will be. There is no birth without pain, no freedom or growth without pain.

Human life could not persist without pain. My wife, who does volunteer work in a hospital for paralyzed veterans, tells me of a young boy, one of the patients, whose lower body is devoid of both motion and feeling. Because he can feel no pain, one day when he carelessly immersed his foot in scalding water, he insensitively left it there, unaware of any danger until he happened to observe that his flesh was literally being boiled to the bone. The result was a dangerous infection which pain, at a cost of momentary discomfort, could have prevented.

When our bodies are invaded by infection, invariably we feel ill. Biochemists have identified the source of our sick feelings as a glandular secretion which they label STH. Were it not for STH, we would feel well even under the impact of infection. But we would also succumb more frequently. For it is precisely the STH which mobilizes our bodily resources against the invader. We would be less fortunate, not more, if our bodies were impervious to pain. And we are victims of illusion so long as we pretend that any faith or device exists whereby a normal man or woman can live without pain, both physical and emotional.

We suffer no less from illusion when we assume that pain is always an inexorable mystery. Often it is; and at best our feeble attempts to understand leave us unsatisfied. But to a far greater degree than we customarily perceive, the sorrows which afflict us can be explained. It is imperative that we pursue the attempt to understand to the furthest limits of our intelligence. For it is not pain *per se* which man finds intolerable but pain which appears to be meaningless. Those of us who have witnessed the unbelievable heights of heroism to which ordinary men can rise in combat and the depths of suffering they are able triumphantly to endure, know that all this is possible because they perceive purpose and meaning in their travail. Their individual effort and anguish fit into a larger scheme which is important to them—the demolition of a blockhouse, the conquest of a cave, the winning of a battle or a war. Tribulations which would have crushed them at home are not only survived but surmounted here. The social morale of the military is only part of the answer, a relatively small part at that. More important by far is the fact that, whether they articulate it as such or not, they see reason and purpose to their suffering.

It is no less important to see reason and purpose under the more mundane circumstances of civilian life. One of the hasidic rabbis has been quoted as follows: "Lord of the world, how could I venture to ask why everything happens as it does? Why are we driven from one exile to another? Why do our foes torment us so? I do not beg You to reveal to me the secret of Your ways. How could I endure the weighty burden of this awesome knowledge? Ah, it is not why I suffer that I long to know, but only whether I suffer for Your sake."*

Here is our ultimate need in travail: to understand that our pains, however piercing or intense, are part of a larger plan, contribute somehow to the fulfillment of a greater purpose. Do they—in fact—or are we only whistling in the dark?

* Martin Buber: *Tales of the Hasidim; The Early Masters*, pp. 212 f. Copyright, 1947, by Schocken Books, Inc. Reprinted by permission of Schocken Books, Inc.

▼ *A Partial Answer*

I believe they do. I am convinced that most, if not by any means all, of the grief we suffer can be traced to one or more of four sources. One: *defiance* of nature's physical laws. Two: *ignorance* of these physical laws. Three: defiance of nature's *spiritual* laws. Four: ignorance of these *spiritual* laws. Let us retrace our steps now to see if each of these can be illustrated.

First, defiance of physical law. A man or woman in the prime of life dies suddenly of a heart attack. Post-mortem inquiry discloses that there have been previous attacks and the deceased had ignored the warnings of nature. Or that the patient had suffered severe discomfort or pain over a protracted period of time but had kept this knowledge from his physician. We know, in terms of nature's inexorable physical laws, that there is a limit to the load any heart can carry; a weakened or crippled heart obviously can survive less than a strong, healthy one. Any course of conduct predicated on the assumption that this is not so is a deliberate attempt to defy nature's physical laws. Sooner or later such defiance is certain to result in tragedy. When it does, the question—why did God do this to me?—is irrelevant.

Much of our confusion and distress is a consequence of forgetting that the physical laws of nature operate with exquisite impartiality. The law of gravity, for example, treats the righteous and the wicked exactly the same. If the most virtuous and the most vicious persons in New York were to jump or slip simultaneously from the top of the Empire State Building, they would fall and perish in exactly the same way. Their fate would bear no relationship whatever to the morality of their conduct. They would be "punished"—both of them—not for evil but for attempting to defy the physical law of the universe.

This does not mean that there is never a connection between the physical and the spiritual laws of nature. If, in the instance just related, one of the men fell because he was boastfully trying to demonstrate his prowess at perching on one foot near the roof's edge, or—better yet—if he lost his balance because he had been drinking to excess, then disaster would have resulted from defiance both of the physical and the spiritual laws of nature. Death from gonorrhea or syphilis is perhaps an even more compelling example. The bacteria causing venereal disease act exactly the same in every human body, regardless of the virtue or vice of the individual. This is nature's physical law. Yet obviously the man or woman who lives a sexually ethical life will be protected by the very law which may damage or destroy the person who is promiscuous. This is nature's spiritual law. Though, in a given instance, the two may be intimately related, it will add to our understanding of tragedy if in this analysis we continue to consider them separately.

Another word should be added before we leave defiance of nature's physical law. It is sometimes supposed that God, because He is believed to be omnipotent, can save us from the consequences of our own folly if only He wishes to. At an earlier point we alluded to God's inability to perform miracles. We mentioned then that if He could suspend His own laws, this would bespeak less power, not more. The same truth holds here. God has established a context of law which enables our men atop the Empire State Building to enjoy the view and descend safely if they conform to that law. Once either of them has so far defied the law as to lose his balance, God can do nothing to help.

After watching her brilliant fifteen-year-old son slowly die of a brain cancer, Frances Gunther suffered the same pathetic heartache that any loving mother would. But she never allowed the anguish of her heart to inundate her mind. Thinking back to her feelings as she beheld the doctors'

vain attempt to save poor Johnny, she later wrote: "I did not
. . . feel that God had personally singled out either him or
us for any special act either of animosity or generosity. . . .
They were helpless, and we were helpless, and in His way,
God, standing by us in our hour of need . . . was helpless
too."*

Rabbi Jacob Shankman has come as close as anyone I
know to summarizing this aspect of our explanation: "Once
in a park I saw a little child running away from its mother.
The mother called the child back but the youngster ran on.
Then the child fell and scraped her knee and began to cry.
And the mother shrieked, 'See, God punished you because
you did not answer me.' I do not believe in that mother's kind
of God. My God does not go around in parks shoving little
children who don't answer their mothers. That child fell because she lost her balance—it is as simple as that, and no
theology is involved."†

This is the easiest part of the problem to understand. When
tragedy results from defiance of natural physical law—deliberate or unintentional—most of us, even in our moments
of deepest grief, can understand that this is not God's fault.
But suppose that death by heart attack comes to one who had
never wittingly suffered such symptoms before? Or—to ask
a question even more fundamental and disturbing—why
should some human beings be born with heart defects or be
especially susceptible to heart deficiencies? The only honest
answer to this kind of question is: we don't know. Or more
accurately and completely: we don't know yet—some day
we will. This is where the second of our categories comes
into play. For remember: in addition to outright defiance of
nature's physical laws, ignorance of those laws can also bring
tragedy.

This is how we must explain the horror of cancer. We just

* John Gunther: *Death Be Not Proud*, Harper & Brothers, 1949, p. 252
† Correspondence dated November 10, 1953

don't know enough yet about the causes of cancer—or of heart disease—or of numerous other malfunctionings of the human body—to assert exactly what nature's physical laws are governing these conditions. But we do know two things beyond the slightest possibility of doubt: there are physical laws operating here too; and some day, we hope and pray soon, we or our descendants will discover them.

Prior to 1955 it was ignorance of nature's physical laws which accounted for the suffering and tragedy caused by polio. Since the blessed discoveries of Jonas Salk our ignorance on this count has been largely dispelled. We are well on the way toward achieving total immunization against polio. When our success is complete only defiance of our knowledge by refusing to administer or accept the proper preventive medication will be able to cause this kind of catastrophe. Once we achieve such knowledge, in polio or any other field, more good fortune by far will come to those who try to obey nature's physical laws than to those who defy them.

Ernest Jones, close friend and associate of Sigmund Freud, reports this illuminating conversation with the father of psychoanalysis: "I told him once the story of a surgeon who said that if he ever reached the Eternal Throne, he would come armed with a cancerous bone and ask the Almighty what He had to say about it. Freud's reply was: 'If I were to find myself in a similar position, my chief reproach to the Almighty would be that He had not given me a better brain.' "*

One can complain—as Freud apparently did—at the inadequacies of the human brain, or one can marvel that so ingenious and creative an instrument has successfully evolved in scarcely more than a split second of cosmic time. Under either option the fact remains that in our own lifetime human

* *The Life and Work of Sigmund Freud*, Volume I, Basic Books, 1952, p. 35

intelligence has eradicated disorders and diseases which only a generation ago appeared to be permanent blights on man's welfare. Which means to say, the area of suffering due to ignorance of nature's physical laws is being contracted almost daily. And the circumference within which we can decrease our suffering by using our knowledge correspondingly expands. So much, then, for defiance or ignorance of physical law.

▼ The Rest of the Picture

Now how about the spiritual or moral laws of nature? Admittedly we don't begin to know as much about these as we do in the physical realm. Where we don't know yet what the spiritual dictates of the universe are—either because we haven't advanced far enough intellectually or because we haven't come even near to using the full potential God has given us—we blunder into catastrophe and sorrow we will one day be able to avoid. Here too, however, it will avail us far less to complain about our ignorance than to utilize our knowledge.

Even now, in the infancy of man's spiritual awareness, we know what some of nature's laws are and we have tasted the bitter fruit of disregarding them. At an earlier point in our exploration we noted the need to love and to be loved, as well as to be honest with ourselves and with others. We may be able to ignore these imperatives with apparent success over the short run but only at our long-range peril. Nature has its way of straightening accounts even with the most adroit of manipulators.

Nature also provides paradigms for our spiritual welfare, even as she does physically. We have already noted some of these. We have observed how, even before the appearance of human life on this earth, evolution tended strongly in the directions of order, cooperation, individualization and freedom; and most prominently, since man's appearance, of development beyond the physical toward the spiritual. Creatures lower than ourselves on the evolutionary ladder have little or no choice about complying with the tendencies of nature. They can scarcely be anything except what they innately and inherently are. Because man does have such choice, he can bring upon himself both higher happiness and deeper despair than is known to any other form of life.

When we ignore nature's compulsion toward order, we reap a grim harvest of cannibalism and crime. When we pretend that nature doesn't strain toward cooperation and love, the consequence is emotional illness and social anarchy and—God and man forbid!—the most monstrous of all immoralities, nuclear war. When we blind ourselves to nature's injunction for freedom, we enslave ourselves as individuals to an infected past and condemn our society to violence and rebellion over two-thirds of the earth's surface. Who can catalogue the full extent of suffering and sorrow due to our defiance of nature's spiritual laws!

There is still more to be said. Any one of us could easily point to instances of intense suffering in areas where both the physical and spiritual laws of nature are known and by persons who have defied neither. The mystery may well be dispelled—though the pain will assuredly remain—if we remember that we stand related to nature not only as individuals but also as members of society and of the human race. We are parts of one another. Both for good and for ill, we are parts of one another. If I am a passenger in a car driven by a drunken driver, my body may be crushed into lifelessness because he—not I—defied the law of nature. By the same token, however, my life is augmented and enhanced every minute of each day because others—not I—have tried to fulfill their highest potential. If it be true, as it is, that I suffer because of others, it is no less true that I enjoy great beauty and share rich treasures of truth and live a longer, healthier life because of others. When I choose to obey or defy a law of nature, I choose for more than just myself.

To complain that this is so makes no better sense than for the paralyzed leg to complain that it has been punished because the spinal cord was severed or for the immobilized arm to resent its disability due to a clot in the brain. We human beings, *all* human beings are related to one another no less intimately or inseparably than are the parts of our bodies.

This must be something of what our fathers had in mind when they spoke of God "visiting the iniquities of the fathers unto the third and fourth generation" of their children. At first this seems to bespeak a cruel and heartless God. But only at first—and only after a superficial glance. A longer, deeper look will indicate how true it is. Our collective moral responsibility extends vertically in time even as it does horizontally in space. The dark stain of one generation's defiance of nature is often written on history's pages in ink which cannot be easily erased. Pain is sometimes the only eventual eradicator.

By the same token, the beneficent effect of each generation's goodness accrues to the advantage of those who follow it in time. The same God—which means to say, in this context, the same principle of moral cause and effect—who visits the sins of one generation upon the next, also shows "mercy unto the thousandth generation of those who love Me and keep My commandments."

The ancient rabbis commented with great wisdom on the statement in Deuteronomy—"Ye are standing this day, all of you, before the Lord your God." *All of you*, they said, means that if there is one righteous man among you, all will share in his righteousness; if there is one sinner, all will share in his sin.

II

The Alternative

What kind of world—which means to say, what kind of universe—would ours have to be in order for all suffering to be expunged from human experience?

To begin with, it would have to be a universe devoid both of law and of life. So much of our heartache is due to those very laws of nature without which there would be no hearts to ache. For example: a human being drowns in the ocean or in a flood. His death brings inordinate anguish to all who love him. The cause of his death and of their anguish is water. The only way for this kind of suffering to be eliminated would be either to have a planet without water or one with life forms limited to those which can survive in water. A planet without water would be a planet without life. An agenda of life which stopped just short of amphibians would obviously preclude humanity. Would even the agonized mourners of the man who had drowned prefer either of these alternatives?

Another illustration: a bolt of lightning strikes an innocent man, killing him. Leaving aside for a moment the question of whether our knowledge of nature might not have been utilized to prevent this tragedy, the only sure way of making such disaster impossible would be to have a universe void of static electrical energy. Lightning, by the way, manufactures something like 100,000,000 tons of nitrogen fertilizer per year—more than the total produced by man. If we had a choice—as we do not—which, so to speak, would be the better bargain: to pay the price of occasional death by lightning or to live in a universe without its benefits? I am not suggesting that this statement of alternatives can mean much or indeed that it should even be voiced to the woman whose husband has just been killed in a storm. But it does serve to illustrate—does it not?—the first necessary characteristic of a universe in which no harm could come to us.

Examples could be multiplied in profusion. Fire, which can burn the life out of us, also warms us and cooks our food. X-rays, which can mutilate our bodies irreparably, also help diagnose and heal our illnesses. Bacteria, which cause the major portion of our diseases, are a simpler form of life without which the more complicated form which writes and reads these pages would be impossible. Without them the amino-acids which are believed to be the elemental building-blocks of the living cell could not have appeared on earth. Without them the food I am about to eat for lunch could not be digested. Which shall I choose then? Bacteria which can both help and harm me? Or no bacteria—hence no life?

Only within our own generation the role of viruses in human distress is beginning to be understood. It is even suspected now that they may have something to do with the cause of cancer. Clearly a considerable amount of disease and pain can be traced to the insidious virus. But so can life.

Our best thinking at the moment seems to identify the virus as a very early form of life or perhaps of not-quite-life. It appears to be a link between the inorganic and the organic, a link without which the one could never have evolved into the other. At the risk of being repetitious if not boring: which would be better—no viruses and no life, or life with all the troubles viruses can cause to it?

Even if life could somehow have appeared miraculously without the potential for pain, it could not have evolved as it manifestly has. A few years ago Dr. Milislav Demerec of the Carnegie Institution presented a paper before the National Academy of Science specifying the probable relationship between the cellular changes which cause cancer and those which produce the mutations on which the whole process of evolution depends. He demonstrated that the same chemical agents which cause cancer also cause mutations. In a sense this makes of cancer an unsuccessful mutation. When mutation succeeds, it paves the way for the next upward surge of evolution. When it fails, it can produce many kinds of misfortune including cancer or even the extinction of an entire species.

Very well, someone might say at this point, it is clear that without law there can be no life. But why can't there be exceptions to the otherwise beneficent rules of nature so that the sharp edge of evil might at least be blunted? Would we really want such exceptions? Could we live very long in a universe whose orderly operations might be altered by the prayers of a human being or the caprice of God? If you, by your prayer, could change the course of an avalanche, directing it away from someone you love and toward a stranger, that same stranger could conceivably reverse the process through his prayer. If I could temporarily suspend the law of gravity for my own weal, that very suspension might redound to your woe.

What all this adds up to is that we can't have it both ways.

We can't enjoy the benefit and security of a universe which is on the whole dependable without from time to time being badly hurt by that very dependability. The only way God, if He were that kind of God, could spare us the evil which results from the inflexibility of nature's order would be to abrogate that order. The medicine, in that event, would be far worse than the malady.

Jewish tradition tells of many who were martyred by the Romans. It is said that one of them, Rabbi Ishmael, suffered such severe pain at the moment of execution that he cried loud enough to shake the very heavens themselves. When the angels on high challenged God to intervene on behalf of one so worthy and noble, a divine echo was heard to say: "If I hear one more cry from Ishmael, I shall return the whole universe back to its original chaos." Upon hearing this threat, Rabbi Ishmael was silent. Apparently he understood that only by a suspension of the laws of nature could he be saved.

▼ *The Cost of Being Human*

In a sense our exploration of alternatives should end right here. If a universe without suffering would have to be one without life, nothing remains to be said—at least nothing from the point of view of human beings who wouldn't be here. But let us allow a deliberate lapse in our logic; let us suppose that life somehow had appeared despite its palpable impossibility. What would then be the character of whatever forms of life there were? Unlike ourselves, they would be automatons. The price of freedom is the possibility of pain. If man is to possess free will, it must include freedom to choose the wrong way as well as the right, freedom to do evil from which he suffers as well as good from which he benefits. Freedom to move only in one direction is no freedom at all. If we want to be free, we must be prepared to pay the consequence of our own and our fellowman's free mistakes. If we insist on automatic protection from all such consequences, we shall have to surrender our freedom.

The analogy of the parent-child relationship has often been used in this connection. I think it's a good one. A sensitive mother or father faces almost daily in one form or another the tension between wanting to protect his child from harm and at the same time to encourage him in growth toward freedom and independence. The parent who becomes overly protective or possessive impairs or destroys his child's potential for becoming a free human being. No child will ever learn to walk unless mother allows him to fall and bump his nose. No one ever learned to ride a bicycle without assuming the risk of falling off or being struck by an automobile. No son ever developed into an independent executive unless father—or his boss—allowed him to make his own decisions, some of which necessarily were mistakes.

This is not just a matter of speculation. Not many months ago I sat in my study with a young man who had come to me for guidance. He had already reached an age at which most men are fathers. What he said to me in effect was this: "I have never been permitted to make an important decision in my life. Whether it be in the choice of a college or the selection of a vocation or even a preference for pleasure, my parents have insisted on making every significant decision in life for me."

I looked at him and saw not a man but the shattered shambles of what could have been a man. I saw not the image of God, but the shadow of his parents' disappointed hopes. I'm sure they meant well enough; they wanted to protect the son they thought they loved from the possible consequences of his own mistakes. But in attempting that they had brought upon him far greater suffering and pain than he could ever have inflicted upon himself.

Is the analogy clear? God too, as it were, had the choice of creating free human beings who would sometimes have to suffer or safe human beings who would never know the meaning of freedom. In a world where we could never bring evil upon ourselves, we would also be impotent to achieve moral goodness. In such a world we would be helpless marionettes, dangling on strings manipulated by a Universal Parent. Perhaps this is what our ancient rabbis had in mind when they explained why God pronounced a verdict of *good* after each day of creation except the sixth day, when he said *very good*. The reason for the superlative, they explained, is that on the sixth day evil was created in the form of the serpent; and good mixed with evil—or better yet, good emerging out of evil and victorious over it, is better by far than good without evil.

A Protestant minister puts this point well: "One can choose protection at the price of growth, or growth at the price of pain. Admittedly, the pain does not guarantee growth; but neither does the protection which sometimes comes from the sacrifice of so great a value as growth offer sure and lasting peace of mind."* Do these sound like glib words? Facile words? Words spun from gossamer threads of logic which would break under the first impact of real-life tragedy? They were written by a man who was born without arms, who learned to write and type and dial a telephone with his feet, graduated from college and seminary, and has held several ministerial positions with success. Not out of intellection divorced from reality, but from the sharpest kind of personal pain, he knows that life without suffering would be life without freedom.

Freedom is only one of the precious possessions we would have to forfeit if suffering and pain were to be obliterated. Everything which makes us human would have to go. A few chapters back we traced the expansion of freedom through levels of existence represented by a rock, a tree, a dog and

* H. Wilkie: *Greet the Man*, Christian Education Press, 1945, p. 94

man. We saw that each stage embodies a new and more meaningful kind of freedom. Correspondingly—and perhaps proportionately—each stage also involves a new dimension of pain. A tree is vulnerable to certain kinds of blight from which a rock is immune. A dog is exposed to refinements of pain from which a tree is free. Man suffers greater variety and intensity of pain than any other form of life we know. But man also experiences levels of growth, of awareness, of creativity which are exclusively his own. An eel never suffers breakdown or bereavement. But neither can an eel experience elegant beauty or exquisite love.

Not only on the ladder of life, but within the human community itself, the two go together. Almost always, greater susceptibility to pain means keener sensitivity to bliss.

A hasidic rabbi understood this well. He said: "Each person experiences distress in accordance with his stature of soul and his work. There is the one who is distressed because of children, because of a parent or a neighbor. And there is one of higher degree of excellence who is distressed over distant neighbors. And there is one greater than he who is distressed because of the whole city. And then there is one, of very noble stature, and he is distressed because of the entire world." Steel refined to the hair-spring of a watch is more delicate and breakable than steel in the girders of a building. China in a Dresden cup is more exquisite and dainty, hence more fragile and frail, than in a coffee mug. The same is true of human beings.

Peter Ilich Tchaikovsky is as good an example as any. He must have suffered as intensely as any man in history. He was a homosexual, an epileptic, an exceedingly morbid man, tormented by such inner turbulence and torture that several times he attempted suicide. The same exquisite nervous structure and tension which enabled Tchaikovsky to compose such unforgettably beautiful music also exposed him to his excruciating pain. The same physical and spiritual endowment which makes it possible for us to enjoy and appreciate Tchaikovsky's music also and necessarily makes us vulnerable to similar kinds of pain. Which would you prefer: a world with suffering and music—or a world without either? We must accept the blessing and the curse together or be willing to exist without either.

I can remember an occasion when my wife and I drove up into the snow-covered hills of southern New Hampshire to visit our friends, Carolyn and Alexander Magoun. Alexander is a man who has suffered a great deal in his life; few of us are more intimately acquainted with agony. He walked through the darkest depths of the valley in 1952 when his beloved son, Richard—in his early thirties—with all the rich promise of the musician, the dreamer and the true man of God—died of polio.

One afternoon we had come in from an invigorating walk in the snow and were sitting together around a blazing fire. We listened to a recording of Beethoven's Fifth while Alexander read paragraphs he had written for Richard's funeral service. We shed tears as we listened—all of us without inhibition or shame. We tasted the full tragedy and beauty of life together. We were drawn by bonds of ineffable love closer to each other and to God.

There was a fifth member of our circle. Carolyn's cat was on her lap. All the while we were there it played with a piece of string. It shed no tears . . . suffered no anguish . . . was aware of no evil. But it also heard no music . . . was affected by no inspiration . . . and felt no love. The alternative to tragedy and sorrow would be at best for all of us to be cats, playing with pieces of string.

▼ *Maturity and Happiness*

There is an almost irresistible temptation, when things go wrong, to seek a scapegoat. When the evils that befall us are relatively mild and within human control, other human beings suffice as scapegoats: a parent, a brother or sister, a teacher or employer, another nation. When our agonies are beyond human comprehension or determination, we often reach out for a cosmic scapegoat. It is then that we ask: why did God do this to me?

An elderly woman at whose funeral I officiated a few years ago never asked this question. She had suffered more than an average amount of misfortune: had been widowed in her forties, buried a son, suffered excruciating disability and pain. Whenever some new mishap occurred she shrugged her shoulders and remarked: "These things happen to everyone; why should I be an exception?"

I doubt whether she had ever read a page of Maimonides, greatest of all medieval Jewish theologians. Yet by her attitudes and actions she shared his perceptive comment, written more than eight centuries ago: "Most of the evil that befalls individuals comes from the imperfections within themselves. Out of these imperfections of ours we cry out demands. The evil we inflict upon ourselves, of our own volition, and which pains us, this evil we ascribe to God."

After all our explanations are exhausted, when we have accounted for all the suffering we can in terms of violation or defiance of nature's laws—physical and spiritual—admittedly a great deal remains. But surely a measure of maturity is the extent to which one concentrates on eliminating the evil which is within his purview rather than on that which remains mysterious. If only we could declare a moratorium on complaints against God until we had eliminated from earthly life every form of pain which is within our power to expunge! God is not responsible for war; man is. God is not guilty of racial or religious or economic exploitation; man is. God is not the sponsor of slums; man is. If we and our immediate forebears had devoted to research for healing and health one-tenth the energy and effort we have expended on more efficient ways of killing our fellowmen, perhaps we would already have discovered the cause and cure of cancer!

Here again a parable from the Talmud is instructive: "There was a great rock that rolled down from the hill and blocked the highway. The people sent a complaint to the palace and the king sent back word, 'Let us remove it together. You chip away at it little by little, and I shall then send and have it taken away entirely.' So God says, 'The evil inclination is a great stumbling block on the road of right living. You do your part and I will do Mine. You break it down little by little and the time will come when I shall remove it from the world."

So much of our search for happiness is doomed to disappointment because it is hopelessly immature. An adult who seeks happiness through methods appropriate for children will succeed no more than one who looks for pleasure in a sandbox. It is of the essence of childhood—and immaturity —to strive after happiness by trying to alter the nature of the universe, to make it conform to the desires of the individual. The mature person understands that his only hope for happiness is to alter himself where necessary to conform to the nature of the universe, which includes, of course, his own nature. Erich Fromm has defined well-being as "being in accord with the nature of man."* The man who aspires for happiness by conforming to the nature of a child, or of less than his highest self, or of a universe operated with magic, must fail.

Can mature religion immunize us from suffering and pain? Certainly not. To suppose that it can is to miss the whole point of this and the preceding chapter. Mature religion is neither a spiritual tranquilizer nor a lobotomy. It deadens no pain and severs no nerves.

What it can do is give us a context for our suffering. It

* E. Fromm, *et al.: Zen Buddhism and Psychoanalysis*, Harper & Brothers, 1960, p. 86

can show us the meaning of our travail and strengthen us to surmount it. By helping us eschew the twin dangers of pity for self and rebellion against nature, it can facilitate acceptance of the inevitable. This is no small service. The person who becomes obsessed by his own misfortune or who defiantly rebels against his fate is like one who manipulates and rubs a wound all day to hasten its healing. The only consequence of such misguided zeal is to delay the very cure he seeks.

The man of mature faith feels no less pain than any other. He may even feel more. But he is able to survive more. He understands and accepts the Chinese proverb: "You cannot prevent the birds of sorrow from flying over your head, but you can prevent them from building nests in your hair." Like one who is in good physical condition by dint of previous exercise and therefore able to recover from injury faster and more completely than one whose muscles are flabby from indolence, such a man heals from the blows of life more speedily and with fewer scars. It is too late, however, to start exercising oneself into fitness after an injury has occurred. And it seldom helps to run desperately to one's clergyman or sanctuary for the first time after an emotional injury has been sustained, begging for immediate relief through faith. Spiritually, no less than physically, our conditioning must precede the emergency. Physical therapy depends upon diligent practice. Prayer is spiritual therapy. The rules are the same.

By the same token, moreover, a discussion of the reasons for suffering, however logical or persuasive, is scarcely the proper approach to one whose heart is in the very process of breaking. It is doubtful whether any words can help under the immediate impact of sorrow. An ancient rabbi understood this when he warned: "Seek not to comfort thy friend while his dead still lies before him." The unspoken gesture of warm understanding can mean more at such a moment than the most eloquent of words. In Alan Paton's unforgettably beautiful novel, *Cry the Beloved Country*, Stephen Kumalo comes to tell his brother John that their sons had both been imprisoned on charge of murder.

> Kumalo comes to him and puts his hand on his shoulders.
> —There are many things I could say, he said.
> —There are many things you could say.
> —But I do not say them, I only say that I know
>   what you suffer.*

Often this kind of empathy is the most effective help we can offer one another in crisis. It will mean more to one who —long before his instant of need—has arrived at a mature understanding of both the happy and the sorrowful aspects of human experience.

I do not believe that God deliberately sends tragedy in order to test or improve us. Yet the sorrows which come to us through the inevitable operation of God's laws can have this effect. We can use them or be used—and broken—by them. Those who are familiar with construction know that buildings contain two kinds of walls. One is a bearing wall; it supports part of the weight built above it. The other is a curtain wall; it divides room from room but carries no part of the burden above. Before adding to the weight of a structure the architect must carefully determine which of its walls are bearing walls and which are not. Mature religion can increase the number of our bearing walls, thus enabling us to sustain, if we must, heavier loads.

It can also encourage us to use even those tragedies we are unable to understand as growing edges for maturity. No sorrow is unmitigated liability if it enlarges our boundaries and our capacity to help others. Even a minor inconvenience can approach the dimension of catastrophe if we allow it to.

* *Cry the Beloved Country*, Scribner, 1948, p. 95 f.

I know men and women who become impatient and impossible if the stock market declines or the evening dinner burns. I also know a woman in New England who buried two husbands, lost three of her five children, suffered major surgery eight times in a period of seven years, contracted crippling polio at the age of forty-seven, limps badly—and is one of the brightest spirits I have ever encountered. There is no limp in her soul. I have never heard her ask why God did things to her. She is too busy doing things for herself and for others.

According to the Talmud, the Holy Ark in the ancient Tabernacle contained the broken fragments of the first set of tablets inscribed with the Ten Commandments along with the second which was intact. I take it this was our fathers' way of asserting that the tragedies of life can be means of growth toward greater maturity and of more devoted service to God.

12

The Door of Darkness Through

Strange, is it not? that of the myriads who
Before us pass'd the door of darkness through
Not one returns to tell us of the Road,
Which to discover we must travel too.

> —Rubaiyat of Omar Khayyam

Whether or not it is really strange that no mortal has ever pierced the veil of mystery surrounding death depends, I suppose, on one's expectations, on his total view of life and death. If it is assumed that individual identity persists beyond the grave and that some kind of communication across the bourn is possible, then indeed it is strange that no message or even hint has ever come from those who have preceded us. But if death is subsumed within the naturalistic religious orientation presented in these pages, it would be stranger and more incomprehensible by far had such communication in fact occurred.

In this chapter, even more than in the preceding two, we come to the heart of man's emotional predicament and need. For that very reason we must not expect to find a single explanation or interpretation of death which will provide security and comfort for all.

Men differ in their reactions to death, perhaps more widely than to any other phenomenon in human experience. I think of two fathers—both known to me—whose sons were killed in the Second World War. The first kept an exhaustive scrapbook, replete with photographs, of his son's every accomplishment since earliest childhood. This was thrust into the hand of each visitor the moment he crossed the threshold and every page was explained with tearful and tedious detail. For months after news of his son's death had arrived, the father dieted rigorously so that he might be able himself to wear his dead son's clothes.

The second father showed me a letter written by his son on the eve of combat. In it the boy had requested that if anything untoward happened to him, the money saved for his medical education be used to provide similar opportunity for someone who would otherwise be denied it. The father had done exactly that. With quiet dignity he told me of the Polish boy whom he had been instrumental in bringing to this country and whose college and medical school education he had already started to finance in tribute to his own beloved son.

I think of two widows whose husbands were both men of extraordinary erudition and learning. One of them—fifteen years after her bereavement—still kept every one of her husband's thousands of books exactly where it had been the day of his death. The other—within a few weeks of her tragedy —was asking me where she might donate her husband's library so that others could enjoy his books and benefit from them as much as he had. One need not be a psychiatrist to recognize in these instances the difference between morbid guilt and wholesome acceptance. Nor need one be a professional theologian to perceive that no one concept of death and its meaning could possibly meet the needs of both.

If evidence were needed of the fact that death touches down to the most sensitive areas of human anxiety, it could come from the frequency with which even modern, presumably mature men revert to superstition in its presence. A frequent phenomenon in Jewish life is the Reform Jew who may not have participated in regular public worship for years but who, when a parent has died, almost compulsively attends daily worship Services in an Orthodox synagogue. Or the man who is moved by the death of his father immediately to enroll his son in an Orthodox school which teaches a kind of Jewish practice from which he himself had departed many years before. Similarly, many Catholics who haven't attended Mass for years will do so rigidly and light candles regularly after a loved one has passed away. Protestants too, under the immediate impact of death, will sometimes turn temporarily to an almost obsessive practice of religious rites long since abandoned. It would be flattering—but scarcely realistic— to believe that such patterns of conduct result only from devotion and love. They manifest at best a generous admixture of superstition. In our reactions to death is to be found perhaps the weakest link in our progress toward religious maturity. Precisely for that reason, this is the point at which we need to strive most zealously for mature insight which will enable us to understand and accept death without recourse to superstition or magic.

The first way-station en route to such insight is a firm realization that death is itself an ineluctable part of nature's laws. Without death there could be no life. This is true in the most elementary sense of quantity and space. If there were no death, in one decade the offspring of a single pair of codfish would fill all the seas on our planet. If all the descendants of an average oyster matured and survived, within five generations they would have produced a pile of shells ten thousand times larger than our earth! Indeed, long before the evolutionary process had come even near to producing codfish or oysters, the simpler forms of vegetation would have overcrowded the earth beyond the point of other life developing or even of their own survival. Quite aside from the fact that life would long since have choked itself into extinction, there could have been no such thing as evolution. For mutations can come only with birth, and without death there could be no birth. Without death life could never have reached the point of speculating on its own meaning.

There will probably be little disposition to argue the point that death, at least when it terminates a normal span of life, is good in the universal sense that everything consistent with nature's laws is good. But how about death when it appears as a rude interruption of life scarcely started? How about death when it comes to a young person or to one in the very prime of life? Here it is no less true—though admittedly much more difficult to accept—that death is a consequence of nature's laws or, more accurately, of an unsuccessful attempt, wittingly or inadvertently, to defy those laws.

The following words were spoken as part of the Funeral Service for a brilliant young man who died at the age of thirty: "Why one so full of promise, so utterly dedicated to creative thinking, to the service of his fellowmen, to beauty and to steadfastness should have died, will trouble many people. I think it would not have troubled Richard. He might have said, 'No mortal man is ever safe from death, for it is not enough to obey the moral law. There is also the physical law and the emotional law. One must obey the *whole* law and somewhere unknowingly I broke the physical law. *No parking* does not always mean *no parking*, and *Thou Shalt Not Steal* is Moses' law. But the laws of the government of nature and of human nature are immutable. No one can ever break God's laws and ignorance is never an excuse. Whenever we try to break God's laws, whether in ignorance or not, we always fail, and sometimes we suffer. Suffering is the chance God had to take and the price man had to pay in order to be able to think for himself. The alternative is to lose all the reliability of the laws of science, all creative ability, all spirituality, all capacity to grow.' "

Will it be protested that this is cold philosophy, void of emotion, impotent to bring comfort to the bereaved? It was, as a matter of fact, written out of the anguished but mature heart of one who at the time was most painfully bereaved, the heart of a father bidding farewell to his own beloved son.* Death, like every other form of suffering, is a response of life to the nature of its own being. Any search for comfort which ignores or defies this truth is tainted with superstition.

Would Alexander Magoun's words bring solace to every father mourning a son? Obviously not. What, then, will determine the matter? In part, the wholesomeness of the parental relationship while both were alive, in part the individual's general level of scientific sophistication, and in considerable part the over-all objectives for which the two persons involved had lived. One's attitudes to life and to death are indivisible.

It may be stated as a rule without exception that any concept of immortality will be meaningful only in the proportion that it provides for eternal survival of that which was most important to a given individual in his life. If a man considers his own physical self and his possessions to be the most important aspects of his years on earth, nothing short of continued individual identity beyond the grave is apt to bring him much comfort in the face of death. To such a

* F. A. Magoun: *Memorial Service for Richard Mann Magoun*, Privately Published, 1952

person these pages will bring little in the way of either meaning or solace, because they are written by one who does not believe that his identifiable body is the most significant part of himself. This hand of mine . . . this pen which habitually falls behind in its race with my thoughts . . . these are not the real "I." It is my ideas which are important—ideas which have come to me largely from many who died long ago, which are now being filtered through my own mind and which, if they are at all valid, will influence the lives of others after I myself am gone. If this is the truly significant part of me, and if there is every reason to believe that this will endure forever, what more do I need by way of immortality?

In short, my immortality consists of my contribution to the on-going process of evolution. This is the purpose of my life, hence the only eternally valid meaning in my death. As I wrote the first sentence of this paragraph, a tiny, delicate, green-colored flying insect settled on my hand. I was unable to identify it by species or name. Yet I know that it is a form of life even as am I. We are both products of evolution. At this moment the life-force of the universe flows through both of us. There will come a time—in the normal course of events, which means to say, if nature's laws aren't violated, to the insect sooner than to me—when both of us will be physically dead. When it dies, there will be nothing remaining, except, I suppose, in the sense that every momentary vehicle of life probably contributes in some small, undefinable manner to the sum total of life. When I die, there will be little or much remaining, dependent upon how I shall have conducted myself prior to that moment.

The insect will live a matter of some few weeks, perhaps only days or hours. I can normally look forward to several more decades of life. But this is not the crucial difference between us. If it were, then the redwoods of the High Sierras, which live as long as three to four thousand years, would be far more significant in the total scheme of things than I. The true difference is that in me evolution has become conscious of itself and its universal setting. I have a soul; the insect and the redwood do not. I can consciously search after the true, the beautiful and the good; they cannot. To the extent, then, that I succeed in enlarging man's total experience of truth, of beauty and of goodness—which means to say, in the measure of my conscious effort to expedite the further progress of evolution—I achieve the only kind of immortality which, it seems to me, should mean anything to a mature human being.

Every normal human being, moreover, can earn this kind of immortality. The ordinary mother whose kindness and love evoke from her child the highest potential he possesses has earned more than a little of it. The businessman who limits his profit to that which can be obtained ethically has gained a share of it. The attorney or physician who hoards a few hours each week to cultivate his love of music or art and invites his children to share this love with him has acquired a measure of immortality too. All of us possess the capacity—in varying degrees, to be sure—to move toward the true, the beautiful and the good. We live on after physical death to the extent that we exercise and develop that capacity.

Even at a time when most men were more naïve about their religious beliefs, there were some who had already achieved this level of understanding. Thus the rabbis commented many centuries ago on the verse in Psalms: "I shall dwell in Thy tents forever." Assuming King David to have been the author of these words, they asked: could it possibly have occurred to David that he would really live forever? Not at all, they responded. What he meant was: may my songs of praise to Thee be repeated in Houses of Worship and study forever!

▼ *One Day Before*

Since death, like birth, is a universal human experience, how can we best prepare for it? How can we anticipate, each his own death with equanimity, and the inevitable demise of loved ones and friends with some measure of composure?

One of the rabbis was curious about the injunction to "repent one day before thy death." Since no one of us can possibly know in advance the time of his death, how is it possible, he asked, to repent one day before? He answered: we must therefore repent every day! The Talmud relates the parable of a sailor's wife who clothed herself in her best garments each day while her husband was at sea. When her neighbors questioned her, she replied: "My husband's plans may change or perhaps a favorable wind will bring him home earlier than he expects; I want to make sure that whenever he arrives I shall look my best." So it is with all of us. The time to prepare for death is each day of one's life. Not in the sense of being morbidly preoccupied with thoughts of death, but rather by so living that death, whenever it comes, will not be cause for incrimination of self.

This becomes especially important in view of the frequency with which the death of a loved one leaves the bereaved with an overpowering and oppressing burden of guilt. Normal grief is a natural outlet for frustrated love. Morbid grief is less a tribute to the dead than an oblation to our own vanity and guilt. The inability to adjust to the death of a loved one even after the passing of years bespeaks something abnormal and unwholesome in our relationship with the deceased even while he was alive. The way to prepare for adjustment to death is by establishing healthy relationships in life.

Within the limitations of a lifetime no person can ever

express enough love or show enough kindness to those who are precious to him. But we can try. Gilbert Chesterton once said that the way to love anything is to remember we might lose it. To awaken each morning with fearful apprehension would be wrong. But it is no less wrong to act as if there will always be time enough somewhere off in the future to show those near to us how much we love them. I remember visiting once the widow and children of a man who had died the night before in his sleep. In the course of our conversation his son, a college freshman, said: "I'm so glad there was no unfinished business left between us. Last night, as every night, we all went to bed lovingly!" There is no better inoculation against morbid grief than so to live that death— whenever, however it comes—leaves us with no unfinished emotional business.

Stephen Vincent Benét understood this well:

Life is not lost by dying, Life is lost
Minute by minute, day by dragging day, in all
    the thousand uncaring ways.*

And if we have been less than perfect in our treatment of one who has died, we must be able to accept our human frailty without allowing it to crush us. It happened a few years ago that within a single week two women came to my study to talk about their recently-deceased fathers. One said: "I hope I have succeeded in giving you a picture of the most wonderful man I have ever known." The other said: "It hurts me to say this, but I lost nothing when I lost my father." These women were telling me a great deal about their fathers but more than a little also about themselves. The second, by her manner and demeanor as well as her words, was demonstrating her ability to accept her own feelings

* *We Stand United and Other Radio Scripts,* Holt, Rinehart and Winston, Inc., 1942

toward her father without obsessive guilt. It is important that all of us be able to do so. Most of us are fortunate enough to achieve this without excessive trauma or the need for professional help. Those who cannot accomplish it alone should be strong enough to seek the help they need.

If healthy preparation for death consists of living as honestly and lovingly as we can, wholesome acceptance of death when it comes to a loved one hinges on returning, as speedily and vigorously as possible, to the pursuit of evolution's goals. People often seek to comfort the mourner by saying: "Time will heal your wound." This may or may not be true. Time, in and of itself, does nothing; it merely gives us the opportunity to do things.

To assume that time on its own account will heal my grief makes as much or as little sense as to pretend that time will grow a garden for me. If I plant prolific seed in fertile soil, then carefully tend the young plants which sprout, time is on my side in the growing of a garden. If I lazily leave everything to nature, time will only propagate a bumper crop of weeds to choke my garden. Time is neutral. What I do with it is what counts.

Time will lead to the ultimate healing of grief only if the mourner turns himself toward implementation of his own highest potential for the further advance of evolution. From this he reaps the double reward of filling his own days with meaning even while compounding the immortality his loved one has already earned in the same manner.

Too many of us, when death has snatched a loved one, delay the first step of therapeutic action, waiting passively for the mood to strike us favorably. This is often a mistake. To some the mood may never come unless a positive though painful attempt is made to induce it. To wait always for emotional readiness to precede action is to ignore one of the most important psychological truths we possess: the fact that the relationship between emotion and deed is reciprocal. True, in the normal course of events our conduct issues forth from and expresses an undergirding of feeling. It is also true, however, that many times conduct undertaken in painful defiance of how we feel can itself alter our mood.

I know this from personal experience. From 1943 to 1946 I served as a Naval Chaplain assigned to the United States Marine Corps. During combat on Iwo Jima I experienced the most intense, debilitating fear I have ever known. There were moments when I would have given almost anything to be able to run or fly away. The very fact that I could not run—that the morale of others depended upon my conduct and there was in any event no refuge to which running would have been possible—the fact that while fearing to the bottom of my bowels I had perforce to act as if I were brave, that fact more than anything else soon brought my fear under control.

The same thing is true concerning grief. Men differ in the time it takes for their moods to change, as they do in the ability to surmount and re-direct their moods. Men are the same, however, in the fact that they need not wait for the mood to change by itself. They can, by taking willful and vigorous action even before they feel ready for it, affect to some extent the way they feel. Helen Keller attests to this with rare eloquence: "Believe, when you are most unhappy, that there is something for you to do in the world. So long as you can sweeten another's pain, life is not in vain."

A young man who from personal experience had learned the horrors of war once said: "Before I die there are going to be a thousand more people who, because of me, feel about war as I do!" A large segment of his immortality is in those thousand people. And each time that one of them performs an act which promotes the cause of peace, he adds to that young man's immortality and the prophet Isaiah's and his own. We remember the deceased most appropriately when we act vigorously on behalf of the goals which meant most to them in life.

Not exclusively but more than most religions, Judaism has placed its primary emphasis on the living rather than the dead. Our *kaddish*, the memorial prayer recited at every public Service of Worship, doesn't even mention death or the dead. The Hebrew Bible tells us that when the first child born to Bathsheba and David was critically ill, David spent the whole night in supplication, refusing to eat. He was so prostrate with apprehension that when the child died his servants were afraid to tell him. But David sensed from their behavior that the child had expired. As soon as his fears were confirmed, he rose from the earth, washed himself and worshipped, then ate. His servants were puzzled over the strange contrast between his behavior before and after the child's death. David explained as follows: "While the child was yet alive, I fasted and wept; for I said, 'Who knoweth whether the Lord will not be gracious to me, that the child may live?' But now that he is dead, wherefore should I fast? Can I bring him back again?"

The rabbis tell us that when David himself died his son Solomon posed this dilemma to the authorities: "My father is dead and lying in the sun; and my father's dogs are hungry; what shall I do?" To which answer was returned as follows: "Feed the dogs first, then take care of your father's body." It was not because they were insensitive to the honor due the dead that our rabbis established this priority but because they were so keenly alert to the importance of life.

When the son of Jochanan ben Zakkai died his colleagues tried to comfort him. "Remember Adam," said one of them, "he too lost a son." "Isn't it enough that I am bereaved myself?" replied Jochanan. "Must you remind me also of Adam's sorrow?" So one by one his colleagues came, each with the same kind of comfort. They reminded him of

Aaron, of David and of Job, each of whom had lost a son. And Jochanan's reply was always the same: the knowledge that others had suffered a similar loss was of no help whatever to him. The last one to approach Jochanan spoke differently. He told him the parable of a man to whom the king had entrusted a precious pledge. So long as it remained in his possession he worried that he might not care for it properly. When the king finally redeemed it the man felt relieved. Even so, Rabbi Jochanan was reminded that his son was a precious pledge. He had taught him all he could and the boy had learned and followed well. Now he had been returned to the king without blemish or sin. From this—and not from being reminded of the grief suffered by others—from recognizing that he had done his very best for the boy and must now continue to carry on for him, did Rabbi Jochanan derive his comfort!

This is one of our greatest sources of solace too when we suffer irreparable loss.

▼ *Childhood Heritage*

Though this is not a book on pedagogy, so much of our trauma associated with death comes from the wrong kind of childhood experience, that a special word to parents may not be altogether out of place. I once had extended contacts with a man who was emotionally ill to the point of being unable to function a considerable part of the time. He invariably plunged into a slough of despondency after the death of a loved one or friend. It was a long time before he was able to tell me about his dreadful experience at the age of seven when his mother died. He knew, of course, that she was ill but had not been told she was dying. One day he was hustled in from playing in the street, told his mother had just died, and cruelly pushed into her room, where he was forced to look at her body. Nearly forty years had passed but death still meant that horrible moment to him.

Few of us, thank God, have had to survive quite that degree of trauma. Yet many of us have been exposed to early encounters with death which were scarcely less damaging, even if considerably more subtle. Perhaps we can spare our children such terror. The first prerequisite is never to tell them a deliberate lie, never to pawn off on them a belief to which we do not honestly subscribe ourselves, never to cover up our own ignorance with a fiction we know they will one day have to repudiate. There is a close parallel here between education in religion and in sex. In both areas a child can at any given stage be given only as much of the truth as he is then able to absorb and understand. This must never be used, however, as an excuse to tell an untruth. We will clearly not be able to give a young child anything like the whole truth, if indeed we know it as adults ourselves. But whatever we tell him must at all times be part of the truth, never something he must later unlearn himself.

The wise parent is never afraid or ashamed to confess ignorance. The secure parent has no need to profess omniscience. It is far healthier for a child to share with his parents both ignorance and a joint quest for additional knowledge than for his immediate curiosity to be appeased by fantasy in the guise of fact. Which means, specifically: the parent who does not honestly believe in heaven himself should never take the easy path by telling a child that someone who has died is now in heaven. The parent who denies or even doubts that we shall ever again see our departed loved ones face-to-face should not give a child such reassurance. Every parent should be scrupulous, in whatever he tells his child, to distinguish between what he knows and what he believes, between what he believes and what he only hopes.

A special word of caution: nothing is better calculated to prepare the way for a sensitive child to become an atheist than to tell him that "God took Daddy away." As adults we can understand "the Lord giveth and the Lord taketh away" to mean that the same Creative Power or Intelligence which makes birth and life possible also makes death necessary. What can these words mean to a little child, however— except that God is a fiend who capriciously robs us of those we love most? How can we expect such a child to love God or even to believe in Him?

The best we can hope to achieve, then, is to use our God-given intelligence to understand as much of the meaning of life and death as may be within our power. Whatever we believe must be consistent with what we know. Whatever comfort we seek must be based on a mature acceptance of fact, insofar as fact is revealed to us. Once we have succeeded in defining our attitudes toward death, we must try to convey them honestly and humbly to our children. Neither we nor they should pretend to complete knowledge. Despite the best of our efforts and after the outermost edges of our competence have been reached, large areas of ignorance and mystery will remain. This is an inevitable part of what it means to be mortal.

13

Talking to Ourselves?

We have yet to examine one of the most crucial questions facing the modern religionist—that of prayer. There are many among us who find it both possible and palatable to accept the foregoing reformulations of religion but who then find themselves impaled on the problem of prayer. If God is conceived as a Person—with magic, supernatural power to suspend the laws of nature, and susceptible to influence by the entreaties of His human subjects—then the value of prayer is obvious. But if we think of God—as we have throughout these pages—in terms of Process . . . Power . . . Intelligence . . . Force . . . entirely lacking the ability to abrogate itself, then why waste time asking for the impossible? On these terms is prayer anything more than talking to ourselves?

The instincts of those who ask such questions are sound.

They realize that the value or function of prayer hinges on how the pray-er conceives God. Maimonides understood this more than eight hundred years ago. He wrote: "True prayer is only possible when correct notions of God have previously been conceived."

For those to whom the "notions of God" developed in this volume are "correct," much if not most of the prayer activity we see around us is puerile. At a time when my niece was seven years old she greeted me one day with this astounding declaration: "Uncle Ro, I don't have to pray any more!" When I made bold to inquire why, she explained: "Because the only things I wanted were a bicycle and a Hollywood bed, and I have them both." The modesty of her demands was far more commendable than her concept of prayer. In the intervening years she has outgrown both. More than a few of her chronological elders, however, still view prayer as a kind of draft on a Universal Bank, a negotiable instrument for obtaining the things they want.

How far removed is this after all from the naïve prayer-wheels of the Chinese? They inscribe their wishes on the blades of paper windmills, then set these out in the open for the wind to turn them over and over until their requests are noted by the gods. Too often we perform with our tongues the same ritual they do with their windmills. In both cases we make of God what William James called "a cosmic bell-hop." One young boy saw through this so perceptively that he said to his minister: "I'm tired of hearing my father tell God how to run the world every morning!"*

Our real concern in this chapter is with those who do not wish to tell God how to run the world or to beg for cosmic favors and who do not believe in any event that their wishes, however eloquently or persuasively expressed,

* Howard Whitman: *A Reporter in Search of God*, p. 161. Copyright, 1953, by Howard Whitman. Reprinted by permission of Doubleday & Company, Inc.

can change the natural order of things. Can prayer still serve as a vital process for them?

I believe it can. I believe there are four purposes of prayer which require no abdication of our intelligence, no diminution of our maturity. Let me list these concisely, then come back to each in some detail.

1. Prayer reminds me of my relationship to the universe of which I form a part.

2. It articulates my true, unique quintessence as a human being.

3. It reinforces my knowledge of nature's laws, of those physical and spiritual patterns of behavior which characterize the universe and myself.

4. It motivates me to conduct consistent with these laws.

▼ *The Universe and I*

Mature prayer should be, first of all, an antidote to indifference. Normally we take far too much for granted. One of the most inspiring prayers I have ever heard was entirely impromptu. I was walking down a country road one rare summer night with a friend. The air was crisp, the sky cloudless and clear, the heavens studded with stars beyond counting. One felt that by stretching on his toes he could reach up beyond the treetops to touch the jewels sparkling overhead. We walked along for some minutes in silence. Then my friend stopped, looked upward, drew a deep breath and softly said: "Thank you, God. Thank you for consciousness of myself and awareness of beauty. Thank you for tonight." Then we continued our silent walk. Neither of us was quite the same person he had been before our pause. Each was more acutely aware than he had been of his natural setting, of his relationship to the other and to the universe.

A similar sense of oneness and of wonder has come to me

while standing atop a mountain, silently scanning miles of valleys and hills, of forests and lakes. Or while floating on my back in a mountain lake—watching white, wispy clouds drifting effortlessly across a deep-blue sky. At such moments there has come to me an ineffable awareness that sky and clouds and trees and birds and I are one—all made of the same stuff—all parts of the same whole—all stages in life's urge to survive and to become conscious of itself. Sometimes my awareness has expressed itself in words; sometimes it has remained an unarticulated mood; at all times, whether verbalized or not, it has constituted prayer.

I cannot climb a mountain or float in a lake as often as I wish. Nor can I afford to wait for such rare opportunities to experience the wonder and awe, the mystery and beauty of my relationship to the universe. But I can seek to re-create such experiences in memory, to recapture under more ordinary circumstances their impact and flavor. Whenever I do this, whether I use the word God or not, I am praying.

▼ *Knowing Myself*

The label used most frequently to identify the primary predicament of modern man is *alienation*. The sense of estrangement we suffer comes, I think, from two sources: we are too far divorced from the rest of nature; and we have allowed ourselves to become so engulfed by the business of making a living that we lose the art of making a life. The second consummation of prayer is to extricate us from both entrapments.

Time was when men needed no reminder of their place in nature. Today, at least in our western world, most of us are more familiar with the sound of motors than of birds, better acquainted with the upreaching of skyscrapers than of trees. We are surrounded and subsumed by massive artificiality. We have just seen how prayer can help restore a balance on this count.

It can aid us perhaps even more toward freeing ourselves from the intolerable tensions of modern living which are sometimes aptly referred to as a rat-race. Apparently this was a problem even under the less complicated social structure of the nineteenth century when the Rabbi of Zans said: "People come to me who ride to market every day of the week. One such man approached me and cried: 'My dear rabbi, I haven't gotten anything out of life. All week I get out of one wagon into another. Yet when a man stops to think that he is permitted to pray to God Himself, he lacks nothing at all in the world.' "*

Prayer can be a man's disciplined appointment with himself for the purpose of being reminded that he is more than an occupant of wagons, more than a rat in a meaningless race. That, alone of all earth's creatures, he possesses a soul. That he has the capacity not only to satisfy his animal needs, but also to nourish his soul through dedication to the true, the beautiful and the good. Even our moments of so-called relaxation usually fall far short of that. When we free ourselves for a few hours from the tensions of the business or professional world, how often we fall prey instead to tensions of another kind: of social competition or television murder mysteries or the search for status. We scarcely have time to get acquainted with ourselves. Prayer provides us with such time.

Rabbi Samuel Dresner has described this use of prayer in terms of his own experience: "When I was a student in New York and lived in the vicinity of Harlem, I often took long walks in that bustling neighborhood full of a thousand surprises. One afternoon, while strolling down its busiest

* Martin Buber: *Tales of the Hasidim; The Later Masters*, p. 210. Copyright, 1948, by Schocken Books, Inc. Reprinted by permission of Schocken Books, Inc.

thoroughfare which resounded with all the clatter of which New York can boast, I was attracted by an unusual sign located among the names of doctors and their office numbers: *Center for Silence. Open from Twelve to Two. Come Up and Sit in Silence.* I was curious and decided to investigate. On the second floor of the building I found a room where men and women, tired of the Harlem jungle, might in silence cast off the stridor of the street and find the peace they so desperately needed. That room was an outpost of repose, a haven of serenity in a world gone mad."*

Prayer is valid if it provides a "haven of serenity" not merely as a means of escape, but for the purpose of re-acquainting ourselves with our own highest potential and —as we shall see shortly—of measuring our achievement in its progressive fulfillment.

So insidious are the pressures of life that even our limited hours of prayer have become contaminated by them. Witness how many even of those who attend our Services of worship rush in breathlessly in time for the sermon, pre-occupied with their mundane worries and tensions as they half-listen, carrying the same weight out with them, un-diminished. Or how many of the smaller number who arrive before the Service commences spend the intervening moments in animated conversation on the ordinary business of life rather than in meditation or introspection. There was once a hasidic rabbi who habitually began his morning prayers several hours later than the accustomed time. His friends, who knew that he was always awake at the regular hour of prayer, asked why he delayed. He replied: "I pray that I may be able to pray."

The second legitimate function of prayer, then, is to afford us an opportunity to become reacquainted with the uniquely human part of ourselves. To remind us that our souls—the margin of superiority which distinguishes us from

* *Prayer, Humility and Compassion,* Jewish Publication Society, 1957

all our predecessors on the ladder of life—are just as much part of and responsive to the universe as are our bodies. Most of us have had the experience of being separated from someone we love for so long a time that we weren't quite sure whether we could accurately recall the look of her face or the sound of her voice. If we allow ourselves to be separated too long or too far from our own best selves, we risk forgetfulness there too. Prayer can remind us of that which we ought not forget.

This bit of instructive dialogue appears in George Bernard Shaw's *Misalliance:*

> Mr. Tarleton: The common people never pray, my Lord, they only beg.
> Lord Summerhays: Then why do you pray?
> Mr. Tarleton: To remind myself that I have a soul!*

▼ *Within the Rules*

We need no less to be reminded by prayer of the laws by which nature operates, of the ground-rules, so to speak, for the game of life. These rules are not made by us; we are made by them. To the extent that they are physical, we who live in a scientific milieu are almost as familiar with at least the more obvious and important of them as with our own names; we seldom need reminding. We are less apt, however, to recall the spiritual laws of nature, and even less than that the directions in which the evolutionary process has been moving. These, it will be remembered, are toward order, toward cooperation, toward individualization, toward freedom and toward the spiritual. It is of these especially that our memories need regularly to be refreshed.

The purpose of such refreshment—indeed, the purpose of

* *Misalliance*, Brentano, 1914

all three functions of prayer thus far—is to motivate conduct on our part which will be more and more consistent with the inherent quality of the universe and of ourselves, which means to say, conduct congruous with the innate behavior-patterns of nature. There are many misconceptions about prayer to be found among those whose religious growth has scarcely kept pace with their increased maturity in other areas of life. Chief among these is the notion, more often implicit than expressed, that prayer can change the natural order or operation of the universe. A major symptom of religious maturity is understanding that the purpose of prayer is to change us, not God; to help us abide by His will, not to cajole Him into conforming with ours. It has been suggested that when the occupant of a small boat pulls on a line connecting his craft to a large ship, he must expect his boat to be moved toward the larger vessel, not the opposite. Often the objective of prayer appears to be pulling a 20,000-ton ship toward a rowboat.

At one point in the play, *Anne of the Thousand Days,*[*] Henry VIII says: "Every morning I go down on my knees and pray that what I do that day may be God's will." How much better to pray first for an understanding of God's will, in order that whatever one does during the day may then be consistent with it!

Some of us remember that after the burial of his little son, Thomas Huxley wrote a priceless letter to Charles Kingsley. In it he said: "My business is to teach my aspirations to conform themselves to fact, not to try and make facts harmonize with my aspirations."[†] Substitute "conduct" for "aspirations" and "laws of the universe" for "fact" and you have the fourth and most important purpose of prayer.

The ancient teachers of Judaism seem to have understood

[*] Maxwell Anderson: *Anne of the Thousand Days,* W. Sloane Associates, 1948
[†] M. Lincoln Schuster: *A Treasury of the World's Great Letters,* pp. 340 f. Simon and Schuster, 1940

this more perceptively than some of their modern followers. In the Talmud they said that if a man's wife is pregnant, he must not pray that the child be a boy or a girl; that has already been determined from the instant of conception. They also prohibit a man who notices from a distance that smoke is rising from the street on which he lives from praying that the fire not be in his own house. This they believed to be wrong on two counts: first, because the fire is already burning, hence a prayer is impotent to change its location; secondly, because to pray for the fire not to be in his house means to wish it in the house of another.

Even the Bible, replete with so many instances of what many of us today would call immature prayer, is not without its examples of the opposite. When Moses finds himself and his people trapped between the Red Sea and a pursuing Egyptian host, he prays for help. God answers him: "Wherefore criest Thou unto Me? Speak to the children of Israel, that they go forward!" In commenting on this verse the rabbis portrayed God explaining himself in greater detail: "Moses, there is a time for a long prayer and a time for a short prayer. The Egyptians are close behind you; this is a time for a short prayer!"

Judaism does not agree with those who cherish prayer as an end in itself and would therefore value a life devoted entirely to contemplation and prayer. It looks upon prayer rather as a means to the more important end of a nobler spiritual and ethical life. Thus the Talmud records a conversation in which the Roman Emperor Antoninus asked Rabbi Judah why it would not be proper to praise God every hour of the day. The rabbi replied: "In order not to mock God, this is forbidden." Antoninus expressed dissatisfaction. Rabbi Judah approached him early the next morning and said to him: "Hail, O lord!" An hour later he came to him again and said: "Peace, O king!" Another hour later he appeared yet again before the emperor, with: "Rule forever, O mighty one!" At this point Antoninus protested: "Why do you mock at majesty?" To which Judah responded: "Let your ears hear what your mouth speaks! If you, a king of flesh and blood, say this when greeted hourly, what shall be said of one who mocks the king of kings, the Holy One?"

All of which adds up to the inescapable conclusion that by far the most important outcome of prayer is action. Without ensuing action, even the most eloquent prayer is like a stage set for a symphony concert—instruments tuned and in place, music opened to the proper score, audience pleasantly expectant—but the musicians' chairs occupied by men who cannot play. The English word *pray* comes from a Latin root meaning *to beg* or *to entreat*. The Hebrew word *pray* comes from a root meaning *to judge oneself*. The difference is crucial. The former is an outworn notion of prayer, incongruous with our present-day knowledge and experience. The latter is a mature concept, consistent in every way with what we know, conducive to conduct through which we glorify God by fulfilling ourselves.

There is a special impetus which sincere prayer can give to improved ethical behavior. It arises from the fact that in prayer there is no need to save face. So often, when we are chastised or even gently reproached by others, we find ourselves bristling with resistance, straining to defend ourselves against what we construe as attack. When we pray, no one is attacking; hence there is no need for defense. No one is even listening as we evaluate our own conduct. If ever a man can afford to be impeccably honest with himself—without need to rationalize or prettify—it is in prayer. This is therefore one of his most promising ways to understand himself with keener insight, to acknowledge his deficiencies in truth and to take his first hesitant steps toward self-improvement.

One of Rembrandt's most illustrious paintings is known as

The Night Watch. For many years it was hung in the great hall of a tavern in which the Arms Guild held its meetings. From the smoke and soot which naturally were plentiful on such premises, the canvas became so besmudged with grime and dust that it was believed to portray the guard marching under cover of night to meet an enemy. Hence its title. One day, however, a zealous cleaning woman applied herself to the canvas. As a consequence it became clear for the first time in nearly three centuries that the scene wasn't one of night at all. The guard was meant by the artist to be seen in the brilliant light of day! The same thing happens too often with our ethical ideals. They become so distorted and disguised by the grime of so-called practical problems that we soon forget their original luster. The ultimate objective of prayer is to clean them off again, to refurbish them, to restore their original brilliance.

The legend has been told of a man who became so round-shouldered and stooped that he walked with his upper body bent over almost parallel to the ground. One day he commissioned a sculptor friend to fashion his likeness in bronze. It was to resemble him in every respect but one: the statue was to show him standing upright and erect. When completed, it was placed in a corner of his garden. Each day thereafter the man spent an hour in that corner of the garden, concentrating intently on the likeness of himself. Each day as he watched, unconsciously and at first imperceptibly he would straighten himself the tiniest degree. Finally he was able to stand exactly as the statue showed him —upright, erect, unbent.

The highest form of prayer is that which shows us a vision of our noblest selves. We pray best when we follow the admonition of Father Zossima in *The Brothers Karamazov:* "Every day and every hour, every minute, walk around yourself and watch yourself, and see that your image is a seemly one."

We began this chapter by dismissing prayer based on magic as unworthy of modern man. Then we asked whether any other notion of prayer is still tenable. Now we have our answer. Prayer is not only tenable but indispensable if it reminds us of our place in the universe, of our unique human proclivities, and of the physical and spiritual framework within which we perforce must operate—all to the ultimate end of so altering our conduct that we may fulfill more and more of our divine potential.

Again the Talmud adumbrates our modern insight: "He who rises from his prayer a better man, his prayer is answered."

14

Can Prayer Heal?

Several practical considerations remain to be explored. For example: how about prayers of thanksgiving? If the most desirable consequence of our devotions is improvement in conduct, is there a place for prayers of thanksgiving? This should seem less puzzling to those who remember what has already been said about prayer as an antidote to taking the good things of life for granted. The late Bishop Lawrence once said he was forced to the conclusion that hundreds of his parishioners must have been lost at sea. This he deduced from the fact that so many of them had come to church to pray for a safe journey, but so few ever came back to express gratitude on their return.

In this respect, most of us are lost at sea. We accept as our due what an ancient rabbi valued more appreciatively: "How much trouble did the first man undergo until he found a piece of bread to eat! He plowed and sowed and harvested, sheaved and winnowed and ground, kneaded and baked, and afterwards, he ate! I get up in the morning and find bread all ready for me. And how much trouble did the first man undergo until he found a garment to wear: he sheared and bleached and combed, spun and wove, dyed and sewed, and afterward dressed himself. And I—I get up in the morning and find a garment in readiness before me. Each artisan arises early and comes to my door, and I find all in readiness.

"What does a good guest say? 'How much trouble did the master of the house undergo, how much meat he brought me, how much wine, how much fruit, and all his trouble was just for me.' But a bad guest says, 'All that the master of the house bothered was not for me, I ate just one little piece of bread, one piece of meat, I drank one little cup of wine. He troubled only for his wife and children!' " Prayers of thanksgiving are in a sense aimed at making us good guests in the universe.

Jewish tradition assigns a special blessing to be recited on seeing a beautiful spectacle of nature. It specifies, moreover, that even a blind person should recite the blessing thanking God for "opening the eyes of the blind" because, though he himself cannot see, nevertheless he benefits from the sight of others. Judaism has never failed to perceive the connection between appreciation and action. He who is aware of his own good fortune is more likely to share it with the less fortunate than he who takes everything as his due. He who perceives the extent to which his welfare is dependent upon his fellowmen will be more apt to serve them in turn than he who is oblivious to their interdependence. And he who regularly reminds himself of the extent to which his whole being is a manifestation of the Creative Power behind and within all things will more probably feel and fulfill his highest ethical responsibilities. Gratitude for our blessings, then, is more than just a mood worthy on its own account. It also is, or should be, the precursor to that conduct which is the final objective of prayer.

One has no way of proving the point, but there are probably more prayers invoked at times of serious illness than under any other circumstance. Does our attempt in these pages to arrive at mature understandings of religion rule out all such prayers for health? I think not. What it clearly does preclude is either of two extremes in the relationship between prayer and health.

The first would make prayer a surrogate for medical science. Or a desperate last resort when medical science seems to have failed. In either event, there is implied an interference by prayer with the natural law. By now it should be patent that no such interference can be brooked by the modern mind. Yet it is sometimes encountered in the most unexpected places. A number of years ago I received a phone call late one night from a physician friend. The fact that he was almost never seen in the synagogue and, so far as I knew, seldom if ever prayed in his private life, is what gives his call its special pertinence. "Rabbi," he said to me, "my brother's wife has been in the hospital now for weeks. She suffers from a strange malady which has thus far defied diagnosis. We have called every special discipline of medicine in for consultation. She has been subjected to every kind of examination or test which could conceivably have any bearing on the symptoms of her distress. But we have been able to learn nothing. We don't know any more about her case tonight than we did when she entered the hospital. All we know is that she seems to be deteriorating rapidly. The family is desperate. We don't want to leave any stone unturned. Since science hasn't been able to help, I called to ask you to pray for my sister-in-law's recovery."

The last thing in the world I would ever want to do is to make light of any human being's pathetic cry for help or to discourage anyone from seeking in religion a resource for strength. But it would be difficult to judge which was in fact more pathetic: the doctor's plea for help or the immaturity of his religion. The implication of his request was that prayer is a form of magic and that I am a more skilled magician than he.

How much more sound was the ancient Jewish view recorded by Ecclesiasticus: "My son, in thy sickness be not negligent, but pray unto the Lord and He shall heal thee. Put away wrong doing, and order thy hands aright, and clean thy heart from all manner of sin. *Then give place to the physician, for verily the Lord hath created him*" (emphasis added). Prayer is not to be accepted as either a competitor or a substitute for medicine.

Neither is the opposite extreme acceptable—that of altogether rejecting prayer. There was a time when physicians —like scientists in general—tended toward a strictly mechanistic view of life. The human body was treated as if it were an enlarged test-tube, different from the test-tubes of the laboratory only insofar as it was capable of producing some of its own chemical components. The maintenance or restoration of health was thus deemed to be little more than the successful manipulation of a chemical experiment.

Wise physicians have long since outgrown so oversimplified and unrealistic a view. Today they realize that a combination of chemicals which produces a specific result in an antiseptic test-tube may not produce the identical result at all in a man's body because something crucial has been added: human emotion and will. These new ingredients can counteract the otherwise normal course of a given chemical reaction or can create additional secretions which are lacking in the test-tube and which therefore change the whole outcome. Anything which affects human emotion or will—as prayer unquestionably can—is a vital determinant of health.

If, then, we reject the view that prayer can replace medi-

cine and the opposite extreme that prayer is of no consequence—and if we continue at all times and under all
circumstances to repudiate the possibility of magic—how
can prayer help us in illness? Our answer will be useful in
the exact proportion to which we succeed in making it
specific.

1. Prayer can give us a sense of gratitude and of balance.
What has already been said with reference to prayers of
thanksgiving in general applies with very special relevance
here. Let a man enjoy good health for forty years and
suffer illness or pain for forty hours; the nearly irresistible
temptation is to forget the former and to be acutely aware
only of the latter. The result then is likely to be either in-
dulgent self-pity or bitter rebellion or both. This becomes
more than a question of character or ethics. In strictly medical terms, self-pity and rebellion are precisely the attitudes
best calculated to prevent or delay recovery. The first and
one of the most valuable contributions of prayer to the
restoration of health is to remind the invalid of all the
good things he has already enjoyed. Rare indeed is the
person whose days of good health fail on balance to out-
weigh the bad.

Two men can sit with identical glasses of water before
them. One complains that his glass is half-empty. The other
rejoices that his is half-full. Both are telling the truth; but
one speaks in a mood which reflects and induces despair
while the other lives the same situation in a context of hope.
Prayer can sometimes tip the balance from the first to the
second.

It can aid toward achievement of the same end by
reminding us of the many others who suffer as much as or
more than we. Again, this is more than an exercise in
altruism. In the same manner that concentration on self
inhibits recovery from illness, concern for others invites and
encourages it. A wise physician who himself suffered a great

deal of sickness has expressed this truth with exceptional eloquence. He is Dr. Richard C. Cabot: "I remember learning gradually, when I could not sleep at night because of pain or discomfort, to pray not for myself but for all those who, all over the world, were unable to sleep. This helps me to avoid tensions and self-pity. I try to imagine the myriad kinds of suffering, physical and mental, that are keeping men and women from sleep. I try to let my prayer reach out to all of them. My own suffering dwindles in importance. When the mind turns away from self, relaxation comes and one holds pity rather than self-pity at the center of one's thought. One gets to thinking of oneself as a private in a vast human army fighting a cosmic battle against pain."*

This restoration of perspective and balance, this emancipation from the prison of self-pity, is the first way in which prayer can contribute to good health.

▼ *Our Allies in Illness*

2. The second is by reminding us that we are not alone. The propensity to feel forgotten and abandoned on the sickbed is insidious. The world goes about its ordinary business with maddening indifference. The sun still shines, traffic continues to move, men buy and sell and argue and laugh —and no one seems to be aware of the fact that I have dropped out of the procession and am unbearably miserable. Ah, but how many people are aware! And how unfair to myself and them to believe that I am really alone!

Often when visiting a patient who is wallowing in self-pity, convinced beyond argument that no one really cares, I have played a simple kind of game. With pencil and pad

* Cabot and Dicks: *The Art of Ministering to the Sick,* The Macmillan Company, 1936, pp. 93 f.

in hand, we begin to list all those individuals who, consciously or unconsciously, directly or indirectly, have made some effort on the patient's behalf: doctors . . . nurses . . . technicians . . . cleaning women . . . researchers . . . relatives . . . pharmacists . . . florists . . . friends . . . Once begun, the list almost defies conclusion. No one still feels utterly abandoned after calculating such a list. Properly directed prayer can help one become aware of his therapeutic allies and almost inexpressibly grateful for them.

3. In another sense too it can aid us to realize we are not alone. One of the unutterable wonders of earth is life's stubborn struggle to persist. A tree, stunted or thwarted in its normal direction of growth, will find a new and abnormal direction. But it will grow. A fox terrier of ours was once hit by a motorcycle. He suffered a severe cervical injury which left him quadriplegic. I visited the dog each day in the hospital and marveled at his tenacious struggle to scramble onto his feet again, to stand and to walk. Even after the veterinarian had given up hope, the dog kept trying. And the dog's will proved stronger than the doctor's prognosis. In the end he did stand again—and walk—and even run! Life had once more been victorious in its perennial battle to persist.

It isn't always victorious. But it always tries. That is what I need so desperately to remember when I am ill. The same life-force, the same urge-to-survive which I admire so in the tree and in my dog exists also within my own body. When I am sick, it operates in a thousand ways at every moment of the night and day. At the threat of infection my white corpuscles multiply and mobilize to defend me . . . If my arteries harden, my heart enlarges in order to possess power enough to push the blood through its narrower channels . . . If one kidney is rendered useless by surgery, the other at once takes over for both . . . When a toxic substance invades the bloodstream, my body at once commences

to manufacture its own antibodies for counter attack . . .
If I need more energy in an emergency, my adrenal glands
immediately provide an internal injection which increases
the sugar content of my blood and redirects my bodily resources to the points of greatest need.

Truly, I am never alone. In the darkest hour of despair, in
the blackest moment of night, when my doctor is gone and
my nurse is asleep and my loved ones are at home, nature
—or God—is acting in a dozen ways I can recognize and
a thousand of which I am not even aware, to rectify the
wrong within me.

When my remote ancestors referred to God as a Healer
of the Sick, they believed he could intervene miraculously
in the orderly operation of the human body to thwart the
course of disease. I believe God works for the restoration of
health precisely *through* the body's order, not *despite* it.
God performs His healing whether I am consciously aware
of it or not. But in this, as in every other phase of human
life, I am God's partner. His success is partially dependent
on me. When I am reminded of our partnership and of His
efforts on my behalf, an important change occurs in my
mood. Trust and hope replace foreboding and fear. My
body begins to secrete juices conducive to recovery rather
than those which aid and abet the agents of my illness. By
reminding me of this, prayer can become one of my physician's most helpful allies.

4. Fourth and finally, prayer can help me capitalize, so
to speak, on my experience with illness. It can aid me in
learning from it, in growing by it into a better, more decent
human being. It can encourage me toward more accurate
understanding and more compassionate empathy for others
who suffer. No accident is it that so many of our finest,
most sympathetic doctors and nurses are men and women
who either witnessed or felt deep pain in their childhood
homes. Illness and pain—like every form of discomfort or

tragedy—can impel one toward either ingrown bitterness or outreaching love. Prayer can be decisive in determining which.

Is all this mere theory—satisfying to the mind but irrelevant to reality? Many wise and competent physicians can attest that it is more than just an exercise in speculation. I remember one occasion when I had preached to my congregation on the healing potential of prayer. Afterward a prominent urologist said to me: "Rabbi, if you were to make my rounds with me tomorrow morning in the hospital, I could show you how far you understated the medical value of prayer."

When he was President of the American Cancer Society, Dr. Eugene Pendergrass spoke of the possible effect of mental attitudes in the control of that dread disease. Among other things he said: "It is my sincere hope that we can widen the quest to include the distant possibility that within one's mind is a power capable of exercising forces which can either enhance or inhibit the progress of this disease."

An eminent surgeon has been quoted as follows. "In operative cases, prayer reduces muscular tension. It reduces the blood pressure and lessens the danger of heart strain which might otherwise be induced by a tense and fearful state of mind. The patient responds much more favorably to anesthesia. For a patient calmed by prayer, in contrast to one inwardly riled up by dread and anxiety, the chances of successful surgery are greatly increased. Post-operative recovery, likewise, is more rapid and more succesful."*

I would not leave the impression that it is as easy for the individual who is afflicted with illness to be balanced and philosophical about his own situation as it is for me, calmly writing these lines while my body and emotions and mind

---

* Howard Whitman: *A Reporter in Search of God*, p. 173. Copyright, 1953, by Howard Whitman. Reprinted by permission of Doubleday & Company, Inc.

are functioning in good health. If it were, prayer would be far less important than it is. A ship sailing through smooth seas has no need for its gyroscope. It is when the sea becomes turbulent that a ship's mechanism of counterbalances must operate at top efficiency. Even so, the restoration of perspective and balance for the distressed invalid can come only through sustained discipline. The discipline best calculated to achieve this end is prayer.

All this is possible within a naturalistic religious orientation to an orderly universe. No magic. No childish begging for exceptions to the laws of nature. Instead, a clear perception of the fact that nature includes Spirit in the universe, manifesting itself as soul within man. That man's physical health is affected always by the condition of his mind and soul; and that prayer can be a very real adjunct to the physician's armamentarium of cures. When we pray for health, no less than when we pray for happiness or for ethical improvement, the measure of our maturity is the extent to which we strive to conform in our conduct and our hopes to the essential nature of the universe and of life.

▼ *And Finally—*

A few pertinent postscripts on prayer may be in order. Like faith in general, prayer will be most useful in time of emergency or need to him who has used it most regularly. It is not a fire-alarm bell which need never be activated unless danger appears. Nor is it a one-shot injection, with a booster required only annually. The value which can accrue from prayer in moments of illness or despair is largely a cumulative value which must be built up in advance over a period of time.

Herein lies the fallacy of the person who, without rejecting prayer in theory, nevertheless neglects any regular resort to prayer for himself. Israel Abrahams encompassed a great truth when he said: "What can be done at any time and in any manner is apt to be done at no time and in no manner." Because they understood how true this is, the leaders of all great religions have decreed regular times and places for corporate worship.

Who of us has not heard someone insist: I don't need a synagogue or church—I can pray on top of a mountain. My reply to this assertion has become: of course you can —when was the last time you did? The person who regularly prays in his home and House of Worship is, I strongly suspect, more likely to pray on the mountain-top also. For he is the one who has prepared himself best to recognize and articulate the fullest dimensions of his relationship with the universe and the discipline through which he can fulfill his potential best. He does not take life for granted—neither on the mountain-top nor in the valley.

There are times when the religious individual wants to be alone with himself and with God. Some of our most meaningful prayers come at such times. But there are special benefits also to be derived from public collective prayer. When we worship together with others we counteract the feeling of futility and helplessness which so often afflicts every sensitive individual. We reinforce our identification with our fellowmen. We strengthen our belongingness within humanity, as a step toward perceiving how we belong, all of us together, to the universe and to life. When all is said and done, a primary purpose of prayer for each of us must be to enlarge his horizons. Both his human and his cosmic horizons. Perhaps this is why the Talmud enjoins: "Pray only in a room with windows."

This is also, I think, something of what Martin Buber means: "To begin with oneself, but not to end with oneself; to start from oneself, but not to aim at oneself; to comprehend oneself, but not to be preoccupied with oneself."*

Let us return, then, to where we started. Does prayer mean talking to oneself? Yes and no. Yes, if we remember that each of us is several selves. In prayer we appeal to and reach for the highest of them. Yes, if we know that part of the ineffable Creative Mind of the universe is within us. Through prayer we address ourselves first to that aspect of God which is closest. No, if we mean talking *only* to ourselves. For the God within is but a tantalizing glimpse of the God outside, as much of the reflection as one tiny mirror can catch of a sun which fills and warms the universe.

* Malcolm L. Diamond: *Martin Buber*, Oxford University Press, 1960, p. 193

15

Journey Without End

If I take the wings of the morning,
And dwell in the uttermost parts of the sea;
Even there would Thy hand lead me,
And Thy right hand would hold me.
—Psalm 139

So we reach a "rest area" in our expedition toward newer understandings of eternal religious truths. Not an end to the journey; there will never be an end—neither for us nor for any generation. In man's restless quest for certainty, each new conquest of knowledge opens out onto new areas of ignorance. We have been climbing through the foothills of religious truth and have now come upon a hillside clearing where we may pause to look out over the valleys already traversed and toward the mountain peaks still ahead.

Several times in preceding pages we have referred to the purposes religion should serve. It should aid us to see meaning in life, motivate us toward worthier levels of ethical behavior, encourage us to realize our spiritual potential more fully and strengthen us in moments of tragedy or sorrow. Though we still mouth many of the phrases and perform many of the rites bequeathed to us by our fathers, these have come to be more and more divorced from reality. Less and less do they truly perform the functions or meet the needs repeated above. Hence the alarming paradox, the pious pretense, of church statistics and shameless immorality mushrooming together. Can our newer insights into religion meet the needs of modern man more adequately than the old? Let us see.

Surely they do help us perceive meaning in life—meaning, moreover, which is at every point consistent with the knowledge yielded by science. We are enabled to see what we are and how we became what we are. As the most recent and progressive product of the evolutionary process, we can compare and contrast ourselves to all the products which preceded us. Instead of quarreling with science, as older views of religion have often felt impelled to do—or fighting a kind of cold war with science by artificially dividing life into separate compartments, one for each—we find it possible fully to accept the results of science, indeed, to build our religious orientation on a scientific foundation.

This does not mean that we limit ourselves to that which science can prove. To the solid line of fact we continue to extrapolate—in the same direction—our dotted line of faith. Above and beyond mere changes of structure and function, we observe in evolution the larger, bolder directions in which the process has moved. And we take our cues from these. We are like men trying to find their way through a thick forest in which there are occasional clearings but no prepared paths. With sextant and compass we endeavor to discover our position, to utilize whatever information is available on the solid line of fact. Then we project, on our dotted line of faith, the course which seems best calculated to lead us out.

Science helps us take our bearings in the journey through evolution. Science and religion together enable us to project the probable future. We see ourselves not as the end-result of evolution but as a way-station en route to something incomparably more wonderful. Biologists may differ on the most crucial single step in our evolutionary past. Some may point to the link from protogene to protozoan, from living molecule to living cell. Others may prefer the advance from protozoan to metazoan, from single- to many-celled forms of life. I believe one day it will be recognized that more important even than these—though clearly impossible without them—was the point at which man for the first time truly became human. That is to say, the step through which for the first time a living creature appeared which could evolve in the spiritual as well as the physical domain and which itself possesses a share of voting stock in the entire enterprise.

Thus, through science and religion together, we arrive at an understanding of meaning in life. We become aware not only of the present as it has evolved from the past, but also of our human responsibility to the future. Neither science nor religion alone can give us this. Only religion founded on science, religion projecting itself beyond science, can succeed. Let it be clearly observed, however, that religion here adds nothing inconsistent with science or contradictory to human reason.

A persistent question imposes itself at this point. Must we not face the possibility that science may be mistaken in some of its present conclusions? Only an affirmative answer to this question can be an honest one. There is always the possibility of error and mistake. Even as Newtonian physics has been in part superseded by quantum physics, and Darwinian theory on evolution has been replaced by more comprehensive understandings, so the way must be kept open for corrections and improvements in everything that scientists now believe to be true. If at any point in the future a new, confirmed scientific discovery indicates that any religious insight now acceptable to us is a manifest impossibility in terms of fact, that insight will have to be abandoned or at least altered. It has been said before that the best we can hope for is a series of religious hypotheses which will explain life *as we know it now*, consistent with the *facts now on hand*.

I would not want to leave this point, however, without stating my own conviction that the kernels of religious truth affirmed in these pages will not be easily or swiftly refuted. They have not only survived the revolutions of knowledge and thought instigated by Darwin, Einstein and Freud, but have been enhanced by them. I believe the probability of future scientific discoveries reinforcing them still further to be of a very high order.

▼ *"To Do Justly . . ."*

So much, then, for the success of our religious orientation in meeting the first of man's major spiritual needs, his hunger for life's meaning. The second and third may now be considered together—the motivation of ethical conduct and the realization of our highest spiritual potential.

Here again I believe the probability of religion's succeeding in its newer garb is very much greater than in the old. Man is now called upon to behave ethically not as a consequence of threats or fear, not simply in response to authoritarian orders, but because this is the whole purpose of his being born and the only sure way of his achieving happiness.

As I write, a major portion of Boston's downtown area is in process of construction for the gigantic Prudential Insurance Company project. To the eye of the uninitiated, the huge excavation is an enormous, confused maze of materials and machinery. If I were suddenly to be placed in the midst of it and told to do my part, I wouldn't know where to begin. Before I could lift a finger, I would have to ask a whole series of questions. What is the over-all objective or plan? What part of the work is now in process? How does it fit in with what has already been accomplished and with what is scheduled to follow? What skills are required at the present stage of construction? Do I possess any of them? Have I—by my nature and disposition, by my capacities and talents—any contribution to make? Upon the answers to questions such as these would necessarily depend the extent of my participation.

If I were told that a subway is being constructed there when in fact it is a skyscraper, even my best effort would hinder rather than help. If I were misled into supposing that a scaffold could carry my weight when in fact it was too weak, I would fall. If I deceived myself into thinking I could undertake some part of the task which requires special skills I do not possess, the result would be salutary neither for me nor for the project at large. In short, only by adhering to the truth concerning the over-all objective, concerning my own limitations and nature, concerning my relationship to the whole, could effective action follow.

In the same manner the possibility of effective ethical action on my part hinges on knowledge which is faithful to fact. It is precisely this knowledge which my newer approach to religion undertakes to give. It induces me to live ethically because this is the kind of life for which I am best suited by nature and disposition as a human being. It is therefore the only kind of life which affords me reasonable hope of happiness. Erich Fromm has come close to saying the same thing from the perspective of psychiatry: "Happiness is an achievement brought about by man's inner productiveness and not a gift of the gods. . . .

"Happiness is the indication that man has found the answer to the problem of human existence: the productive realization of his potentialities and thus, simultaneously, being one with the world and preserving the integrity of his self. . . .

"Man's main task in life is to give birth to himself, to become what he potentially is."*

The search after material possessions, after status or prestige or power, can bring me pleasure or enjoyment but never happiness. This, because the search after such as these is not consistent with my true nature as a man. Back in 1952 there were radio news reports of a dog which sat stubbornly near the top of a well for sixteen hours. Not even the call of his master could move him. Worried that perhaps a child had fallen into the well and the dog was calling attention to its plight, a crew of men worked for many hours to reach the bottom of the well—only to find there a bone the dog had dropped! A dog, yearning after a little bone, acts true to its nature; it can be "happy." A man, yearning only after the larger bones of material possession or power, is faithless to his true nature; real happiness will elude him.

If an American-manufactured electric shaver is plugged into the higher voltage of European current, it will not operate. Before it can be used, a transformer plug must change the European current into the lower American voltage. The shaver must be operated on electric current suited to its own nature. A man who tries to operate on lower ethical voltage than that of his true nature can never find abiding happiness.

In short, my modern religious orientation convinces me that I must live ethically because only thus can I live happily. I may succeed in cheating the professor of a class on an ex-

* *Man for Himself*, Holt, Rinehart and Winston, Inc., 1947, pp. 189, 237

amination or the government by falsifying my tax return, but I can never successfully cheat myself. I am the one to be hurt most deeply by disregarding my own nature. If men will not behave ethically for this reason, they will not behave ethically at all.

What has been said of the good is equally applicable to the beautiful and the true. Because I have the capacity to seek and express both, I shall never be happy unless I do. A race horse, permanently penned in a small space, deprived of all opportunity to run, would soon lose its speed. It might continue for a long or a short time to vegetate; in no true sense of the word could it be said still to be living. No less is true of a human being, deprived of the opportunity to create or appreciate beauty, to seek and acknowledge truth. The assurance that thus do I best fulfill the cosmic purpose of my life increases the probability that I shall continue the pursuit.

What about the fourth purpose of religion—to act as a shock-absorber in man's inevitable passage over the bumps of life? Is the newer approach to religion more likely to succeed here than the old? I would say *yes*. For one thing, it obviates the old dilemma posed by Nickles in *J.B.*

If God is God He is not good.
If God is good He is not God.*

The newer understanding of religion allows God to be both God and good. It does not blink the existence of evil, both within man and outside him. It accepts the reality of pain and shows man the meaning of his sorrow. It accounts for his suffering in a world of reality, not one of illusion.

If I am encouraged to believe—as I am by the old ways—that God can spare me all pain if He wishes to and if I am deserving, then His failure to do so leaves me with the inescapable conclusion that there must be something radically

* Archibald MacLeish: *J. B.*, Houghton Mifflin Company, 1958, p. 11

wrong either with God or with me. My new road to religion enables me to separate my suffering into two categories: that which can be and therefore should be eradicated through human effort; and that which at least up to the present moment is beyond our ability to affect, which we must learn to accept and to use. In neither case is it necessary to compound my anguish with guilt.

On all counts, then—in clarifying the meaning of life, in persuading me toward greater fulfillment of my uniquely human potential, and in preparing me to endure pain—a concept of religion and of God appropriate for the twentieth century is more likely to function in my life successfully than one suited for the twelfth.

▼ Heart and Head

An important question remains. Is all this a series of cold abstractions, remote from man's heart even if satisfying to his head? The answer must depend on who is asking. There are undoubtedly large numbers of people who can be comforted and encouraged only by a simpler, more personalized kind of faith, who feel like orphans of the universe unless God is a Cosmic Papa. These should be neither denied nor decried. For as long into the future as our vision can at present penetrate, there will be religious leaders and institutions of many varieties to meet their needs. Though, at the moment, the numbers may be smaller of those who can no longer give more than lip-service, if that, to the old religious patterns, they too are deserving of attention. It is for them that these chapters have been written.

For myself, there is nothing cold or abstract about glimpsing my role in the great cosmic adventure of life. I feel the deepest, warmest kind of stirring within me when I listen to the Shostakovitch Fifth and reflect that this ineffable beauty is what man—product of protozoan though he be—is now capable of creating and appreciating. My heart beats faster with excitement when I stand on a New England knoll in October, breathing in the glorious colors of leaves and somehow sensing that they and I alike are manifestations of a universal life-force which unites us. I can tremble with excitement at the dawn in my mind of a new truth, knowing that it makes me partner to every searcher for truth from the beginning of time and relates me intimately to the ultimate Source of Truth. I have been moved almost to tears by the realization that a turbulent struggle within me, followed by the choice of an ethically good act instead of its evil alternative, was my way of saying *yes* to God, of becoming truly His creative partner on earth. Cold and abstract? For me, nothing in human experience can be warmer or more immediate.

It would be too much to expect that everyone would feel the same. In religion, as in all other areas of life, we stand on varying levels of comprehension and need. We must seek —each of us—a kind of religious orientation congenial to himself, to his best and highest self. This is mine. I make bold to believe that it is more than mine, that it anticipates the religious direction of the future. I am convinced that if not we, our children—and if not they, our grandchildren— will be ready for concepts such as these. The result, I dare to hope, will be men and women of richer maturity, a human race which will succeed in resembling more closely than we the image of God.

The long day of human achievement has scarcely begun. Compared to the incalculable aeons of astronomic and geologic time, man has occupied the earth only a few seconds. Our accomplishments of the past are as nothing when measured against our hopes for the future. There will come a day when our capacity to understand life and to live it creatively will have advanced so far that even the concepts of this volume—so radical and disturbing to some—will be discarded as outgrown. The dawn of that day is part of God's plan. It will surely come—*if man does his share.*

The sun is up. The day has commenced. We soar on the wings of the morning.

Index

ABOUT THE AUTHOR

ROLAND B. GITTELSOHN has been Rabbi of Temple Israel in Boston since 1953. From 1936 to 1953 he was Rabbi of the Central Synagogue of Nassau County, Long Island. A past president of the Massachusetts Board of Rabbis, he has held important posts with the Central Conference of American Rabbis and with the Union of American Hebrew Congregations, of which he is a trustee. He has served on President Truman's Committee on Civil Rights, on the Governor's Commission to Survey Massachusetts Courts, and on the Massachusetts Commission on Abolition of the Death Penalty.

A graduate of Western Reserve University and Hebrew Union College, Rabbi Gittelsohn has done graduate work at Teacher's College, Columbia University. In June, 1961, he received an honorary Doctor of Divinity degree from Hebrew Union College and an honorary Doctor of Science degree from the Lowell Technological Institute. During World War II he served as a chaplain with the U.S. Naval Reserves. He was awarded three ribbons for the campaign of Iwo Jima, and delivered the dedicatory sermon at the Fifth Marine Division Cemetery there.

Rabbi Gittelsohn is the author of *Modern Jewish Problems* and *Little Lower than the Angels,* textbooks in contemporary Jewish life and Jewish theology, respectively, for high school classes in Jewish religious schools.